Data Visualization with d3.js

Mold your data into beautiful visualizations with d3.js

Swizec Teller

PUBLISHING

BIRMINGHAM - MUMBAI

Data Visualization with d3.js

First published: October 2013

Production Reference: 1181013

Published by Packt Publishing Ltd.
Livery Place
35 Livery Street
Birmingham B3 2PB, UK.

ISBN 978-1-78216-000-7

www.packtpub.com

Cover Image by Ravaji Babu (ravaji_babu@outlook.com)

Credits

Author
Swizec Teller

Reviewers
Kamal Marhubi

Pablo Navarro

Kent Russell

Acquisition Editor
Wilson D'souza

Commissioning Editors
Llewellyn Rozario

Poonam Jain

Technical Editors
Veena Pagare

Manal Pednekar

Copy Editors
Alisha Aranha

Roshni Banerjee

Brandt D'Mello

Gladson Monteiro

Adithi Shetty

Project Coordinator
Esha Thakker

Proofreader
Kevin McGowan

Indexer
Tejal R.Soni

Graphics
Ronak Dhruv

Abhinash Sahu

Production Coordinator
Nitesh Thakur

Cover Work
Nitesh Thakur

About the Author

Swizec Teller is a geek with a hat. Founding his first startup at 21, he is now looking for the next big idea as a full-stack web generalist focusing on freelancing for early-stage startup companies.

When he isn't coding, he's usually blogging, writing books, or giving talks at various non-conference events in Slovenia and nearby countries. He is still looking for a chance to speak at a big international conference.

In November 2012, he started writing *Why Programmers Work at Night*, and set out on a quest to improve the lives of developers everywhere.

I want to thank @gandalfar and @robertbasic for egging me on while writing and being my guinea pigs for the examples. I also want to send love to everyone at @psywerx for keeping me sane and creating one of the best datasets ever.

About the Reviewers

Pablo Navarro is a data visualization consultant from Chile. He earned his Masters degree in Applied Mathematics from École des Mines de Saint-Etienne, France. After working for some years in operations research and data analysis, he decided to specialize in data visualization for web platforms, in which he currently works. In his free time, he enjoys doing watercolor illustrations, running, and reading about human evolution. His most recent works can be seen at `http://pnavarrc.github.io`.

Kent Russell is an investment manager passionate about data visualization

www.PacktPub.com

Support files, eBooks, discount offers and more

You might want to visit www.PacktPub.com for support files and downloads related to your book.

Did you know that Packt offers eBook versions of every book published, with PDF and ePub files available? You can upgrade to the eBook version at www.PacktPub.com and as a print book customer, you are entitled to a discount on the eBook copy. Get in touch with us at service@packtpub.com for more details.

At www.PacktPub.com, you can also read a collection of free technical articles, sign up for a range of free newsletters and receive exclusive discounts and offers on Packt books and eBooks.

http://PacktLib.PacktPub.com

Do you need instant solutions to your IT questions? PacktLib is Packt's online digital book library. Here, you can access, read and search across Packt's entire library of books.

Why Subscribe?

- Fully searchable across every book published by Packt
- Copy and paste, print and bookmark content
- On demand and accessible via web browser

Free Access for Packt account holders

If you have an account with Packt at www.PacktPub.com, you can use this to access PacktLib today and view nine entirely free books. Simply use your login credentials for immediate access.

Table of Contents

Preface

When learning d3.js on your own, there is often a feeling of *Step 1: Draw two circles, Step 2: Draw the rest of the owl*. This book tries to bridge that gap.

It uses complete examples that take you from basic shapes on a page to full-blown examples. There is no magic here, no steps are left unexplained. You will understand everything that goes into making a visualization with d3.js.

We'll touch everything from manipulating data to make it easier to work with, to using advanced features to separate drawing from calculating coordinates.

What this book covers

Chapter 1, Getting Started with d3.js, gives a simple example to show you the basics of d3.js and helps you to set up a common environment, which is used throughout the rest of the book.

Chapter 2, A Primer on DOM, SVG, and CSS, explains in detail how to use d3.js for manipulating content on a page, paying special attention to SVG and the core tools for creating images.

Chapter 3, Making Data Useful, shows you how to manipulate data in a functional manner, load data from external sources, and use the built-in tools of d3.js to avoid tedious coding.

Chapter 4, Making Things Move, talks about animating visualizations with d3.js and allowing users to interact with your images.

Chapter 5, Layouts – d3's Black Magic, explains how d3.js layouts work and shows you how to use the same dataset to get vastly different images. The fancy visualizations out there will no longer look like magic.

Chapter 6, Designing Good Visualizations, looks at a few examples of great visualizations from around the web and discusses just what it is that makes them great.

What you need for this book

You don't need much to play along with the examples. A machine geared for web development will have everything.

We assumed the Chrome browser in the examples, but everything should work in Safari, Firefox, and Internet Explorer Version 10 and above. The specific browser only affects how your debugging tools work, but they're very similar in all browsers anyway.

We also use Python to run a small server. If you're using Mac or Linux, Python is already installed; otherwise, you've to get a version. The only thing we ever do with Python is run a single command.

And lastly, you are going to need a text editor. Personally I like Emacs, but Sublime and Notepad++ are also popular choices. Yes, you can use Vim too.

Who this book is for

This book is for everyone who's tried learning d3.js on their own, looked at a few examples and thought: "What the hell is this magic?".

The book assumes you've written some JavaScript before, are relatively comfortable with web development in general, have a firm grasp of programming basics, and have looked at d3.js examples before. By the end of this book, you will be able to understand code from even the fanciest visualizations.

Conventions

In this book, you will find a number of styles of text that distinguish between different kinds of information. Here are some examples of these styles, and an explanation of their meaning.

Code words in text, database table names, folder names, filenames, file extensions, pathnames, dummy URLs, user input, and Twitter handles are shown as follows: "At the end, we include a `code.js` file where we'll put most of our code "

A block of code is set as follows:

```
data = d3.keys(data).map(function (key) {
    return {bucket: Number(key),
      N: data[key]};
    });
```

Any command-line input or output is written as follows:

```
> topojson -o water.json ne_50m_rivers_lake_centerlines.shp ne_50m_ocean.shp
> topojson -o land.json ne_50m_land.shp
> topojson -o cultural.json ne_50m_admin_0_boundary_lines.shp ne_10m_urban_areas.shp
```

New terms and **important words** are shown in bold. Words that you see on the screen, in menus or dialog boxes for example, appear in the text like this: " You'll find them in the **Downloads** tab".

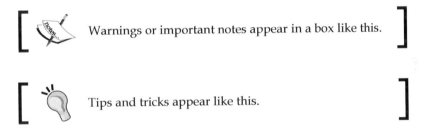

Warnings or important notes appear in a box like this.

Tips and tricks appear like this.

Reader feedback

Feedback from our readers is always welcome. Let us know what you think about this book—what you liked or may have disliked. Reader feedback is important for us to develop titles that you really get the most out of.

To send us general feedback, simply send an e-mail to feedback@packtpub.com and mention the book title via the subject of your message.

If there is a topic that you have expertise in and you are interested in either writing or contributing to a book, see our author guide on www.packtpub.com/authors.

Customer support

Now that you are the proud owner of a Packt book, we have a number of things to help you to get the most from your purchase.

Downloading the example code

You can download the example code files for all Packt books you have purchased from your account at http://www.packtpub.com. If you purchased this book elsewhere, you can visit http://www.packtpub.com/support and register to have the files e-mailed directly to you.

Downloading the color images of this book

We also provide you with a PDF file that has color images of the screenshots used in this book. You can download this file from http://www.packtpub.com/sites/default/files/downloads/0007OS_Images.pdf.

Errata

Although we have taken every care to ensure the accuracy of our content, mistakes do happen. If you find a mistake in one of our books—maybe a mistake in the text or the code—we would be grateful if you would report this to us. By doing so, you can save other readers from frustration and help us improve subsequent versions of this book. If you find any errata, please report them by visiting http://www.packtpub.com/submit-errata, selecting your book, clicking on the **errata submission form** link, and entering the details of your errata. Once your errata are verified, your submission will be accepted and the errata will be uploaded on our website, or added to any list of existing errata, under the Errata section of that title. Any existing errata can be viewed by selecting your title from http://www.packtpub.com/support.

Piracy

Piracy of copyright material on the Internet is an ongoing problem across all media. At Packt, we take the protection of our copyright and licenses very seriously. If you come across any illegal copies of our works, in any form, on the Internet, please provide us with the location address or website name immediately so that we can pursue a remedy.

Please contact us at `copyright@packtpub.com` with a link to the suspected pirated material.

We appreciate your help in protecting our authors, and our ability to bring you valuable content.

Questions

You can contact us at `questions@packtpub.com` if you are having a problem with any aspect of the book, and we will do our best to address it.

1

Getting Started with d3.js

In this chapter, I'll show you the basic tools for making simple visualizations in d3.js without going into too much depth so that you can get started immediately. We will go through the basic language of d3.js and also its rules.

We'll take a stab at creating axes and automatically scaling graphs to fit the viewport, and learn about using Chrome Developer Tools to model our code before going into a full-blown programming bonanza. Through this chapter, we're going to set up the environment used throughout the book and create an animated chart of a dataset I created from GitHub.

What is d3.js?

The name D3 stands for Data-Driven Documents. *Mike Bostock* has been openly developing this powerful data visualization library since 2011. It helps you draw beautiful graphics by manipulating data without worrying too much about pixel positions, calculating where things fit on a graph, and so on. If you've ever visualized data in Python or similar languages, you've probably used something similar to **gnuplot**. I assure you that d3.js offers a much more pleasurable experience.

The official website, d3js.org, features many great examples that show off the power of d3.js, but understanding them is tricky at best. After finishing this book, you should be able to understand d3.js well enough to figure out the examples. If you want to follow the development of d3.js more closely, the source code is hosted on GitHub at https://github.com/mbostock/d3.

The fine-grained control and its elegance make d3.js one of the most, if not the most, powerful open source visualization libraries out there. This also means that it's not very suitable for simple jobs such as drawing a chart or two—in that case you might want to use a library designed for charting. Many use d3.js internally anyway.

As a data manipulation library, d3.js is based on functional programming principles, which is probably where a lot of the confusion stems from. Unfortunately, functional programming goes beyond the scope of this book, but I'll explain all the relevant bits to make sure everyone's on the same page.

Setting up a play environment

D3 combines HTML, CSS, and SVG to create graphics. That means we're going to need an HTML and a JavaScript file. We'll use Chrome Developer Tools to tweak our visualizations and test things out. Let's start with some HTML coding:

```
<!DOCTYPE html>
<title></title>
<link href="bootstrap/css/bootstrap.min.css" rel="stylesheet">

<div id="graph"></div>

<script src="http://d3js.org/d3.v3.min.js"></script>
<script src="code.js"></script>
```

These six lines of HTML code are the basics we're going to use throughout this book.

The first two lines comprise a minimal HTML5 document. You no longer need to include the `<html>`, `<head>`, and `<body>` tags. Next is the `<link>` tag that pulls in Twitter Bootstrap's CSS rules—a good set of defaults to make things prettier. After that comes the `<div>` tag that will hold our visualization, and finally, there's the `<script>` tag that loads d3.js.

At the end, we include a `code.js` file, where we'll put most of our code. Twitter doesn't offer a hosted version of Bootstrap, so you have to download the whole package from `http://twitter.github.com/bootstrap/` and unpack it next to the other files you're working with. All we need now is a server to run everything. This is because we don't want to get into trouble with browser security models when making Ajax requests. Any server will do, but here's a quick way to get one up and running if you already have Python installed (by default on Mac and Linux).

Fire up a console, navigate to your working directory, and run the following command:

```
$ python -m SimpleHTTPServer
```

Python will run the `SimpleHTTPServer` module as a standalone script and create a fully functional local server.

Now point Chrome to `localhost:8000` and fire up the developer console—*Ctrl + Shift + J* for Linux and Windows and *Option + Command + J* for Mac. You should see a blank website and a blank JavaScript console with a command prompt waiting for some code:

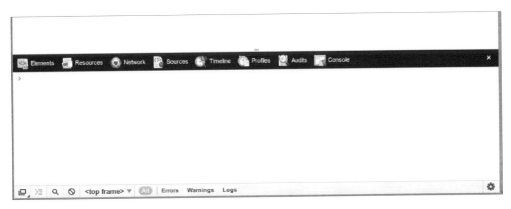

A quick Chrome Developer Tools primer

Chrome Developer Tools are indispensable in web development. Most modern browsers have something similar, but I thought we'd stick to a single example to keep the book shorter. Feel free to use a different browser.

We are mostly going to use the **Elements** and **Console** tabs: **Elements** to inspect the DOM, and **Console** to play with JavaScript code and look for any problems.

The other six tabs come in handy for large projects. The **Network** tab will let you know how long files are taking to load and helps you inspect the Ajax requests. The **Profiles** tab will help you profile JavaScript for performance. The **Resources** tab is good for inspecting client-side data. Honestly, I have never needed **Timeline** and **Audits** before. One of the favorites from Developer Tools is the CSS inspector at the right-hand side of the **Elements** tab.

It can tell you what CSS rules are affecting the styling of an element, which is very good for hunting rogue rules that are messing things up. You can also edit the CSS and immediately see the results:

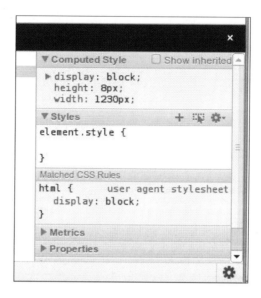

A simple histogram

We'll go through the basics of d3.js by creating a histogram indicating when the GitHub users commit code. We're going to label axes, make sure things are scalable, and modify animations for that extra bit of flair.

The dataset contains 504,015 repositories and it took me a week to create it out of punchcard data for each repository. A punchcard is just a 7 x 24 grid of buckets, specifying how many commits happened within a specific day and hour. The dataset's histogram digest is hosted at http://nightowls.swizec.com/data/histogram-hours.json and maps hours to the sum of commits occurring within that hour.

This is what we're aiming for:

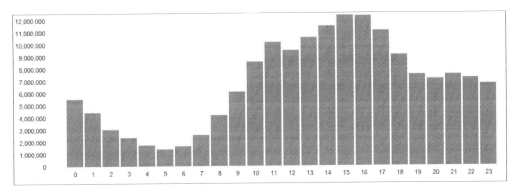

We begin by taking the environment prepared in the previous section and adding a few lines around the central `<div>` tag:

```
<div class="container">
  <div class="row">
    <div id="graph" class="span12"></div>
  </div>
</div>
```

The extra `<div>` tags center the graph horizontally and ensure that we have 900 px of width to work with. Don't forget to add the `class="span12"` parameter into the `graph` div. It tells Bootstrap the div should go the whole width of the grid.

To avoid tripping your browser's security restrictions regarding cross-domain requests, you should now take a moment to download the dataset and save it next to the other files. Remember, it's at `http://nightowls.swizec.com/data/histogram-hours.json`.

You can play around with the following code in Chrome Developer Tools to see what it does and then save it in `code.js`. Writing directly to the file also works, but just make sure you refresh frequently. Learning is if you know what each line does.

We begin with some variables as follows:

```
var width = 900, height = 300, pad = 20, left_pad = 100;
```

We're going to use these to specify the dimensions of our drawing area. The `pad` variable will define the padding from the edge, with `left_pad` giving a bigger margin on the left to allow for labels.

Next, we define a horizontal scale, x:

```
var x = d3.scale.ordinal().rangeRoundBands([left_pad, width - pad],
    0.1);
```

The x scale is now a function that maps inputs from a yet unknown domain (we don't have the data yet) to a range of values between `left_pad` and `width - pad`, that is, between `100` and `880` with some spacing defined by the `0.1` value. Because it's an ordinal scale, the domain will have to be discrete rather than continuous. `rangeRoundBands` means the range will be split into bands that are guaranteed to be round numbers.

Then, we define another scale named y:

```
var y = d3.scale.linear().range([height-pad, pad]);
```

Similarly, the y scale is going to map a yet unknown linear domain to a range between `height-pad` and `pad`, that is, `880` and `20`. Inverting the range is important because d3.js considers the top of a graph to be y=0.

Now, we define our axes as follows:

```
var xAxis = d3.svg.axis().scale(x).orient("bottom");
var yAxis = d3.svg.axis().scale(y).orient("left");
```

We've told each axis what scale to use when placing ticks and which side of the axis to put the labels on. D3 will automatically decide how many ticks to display, where they go, and how to label them.

The last step before loading the data is defining an SVG element for the histogram:

```
var svg = d3.select("#graph").append("svg")
            .attr("width", width).attr("height", height);
```

Switching quickly to the **Elements** tab, you'll notice a new HTML element with a width of 900 and a height of 100.

Now the fun begins!

We're going to use d3.js itself to load data remotely and then draw the graph in the callback function. Remember to use *Shift + Enter* to input multiline code in the Chrome console. Now might be a good time to switch to coding in `code.js` directly and refreshing after every couple of steps:

```
d3.json('histogram-hours.json', function (data) {
});
```

`d3.json` will create an Ajax request to load a JSON file, then parse the received text into a JavaScript object. D3 understands CSV and some other data formats as well, which is kind of awesome if you ask me.

From here on, we put everything in that callback function (before the `});` bit). Our data will be in the `data` variable. D3 is a functional data-munging library, so we need to transform our dictionary data into a list of simple objects. We do this using the following code:

```
data = d3.keys(data).map(function (key) {
  return {bucket: Number(key),
    N: data[key]};
});
```

`d3.keys` returns a list of keys in the data dictionary, which we then `map` over with an iterator function that returns a simple dictionary for every item. It tells us where an item fits in the histogram (`bucket`) and what value it holds (`N`).

We've turned our data into a list of two-value dictionaries.

Remember the `x` and `y` scales from before? We can finally give them a domain and make them useful:

```
x.domain(data.map(function (d) { return d.bucket; }));
y.domain([0, d3.max(data, function (d) { return d.N; })]);
```

Since most d3.js elements are objects and functions at the same time, we can change the internal state of both scales without assigning the result to anything. The domain of `x` is a list of discrete values. The domain of `y` is a range from `0` to `d3.max` of our dataset—the largest value.

Now we're going to draw the axes on our graph:

```
svg.append("g")
  .attr("class", "axis")
  .attr("transform", "translate(0, "+(height-pad)+")")
  .call(xAxis);
```

We've appended an element called g to the graph, given it the CSS class "axis", and moved the element to a place at the bottom-left of the graph with the transform attribute.

Finally, we call the xAxis function and let d3.js handle the rest.

Drawing the other axis works exactly the same, but with different arguments:

```
svg.append("g")
  .attr("class", "axis")
  .attr("transform", "translate("+(left_pad-pad)+", 0)")
  .call(yAxis);
```

Now that our graph is labeled, it's finally time to draw some data:

```
svg.selectAll('rect')
  .data(data)
  .enter()
  .append('rect')
  .attr('class', 'bar')
  .attr('x', function (d) { return x(d.bucket); })
  .attr('width', x.rangeBand())
  .attr('y', function (d) { return y(d.N); })
  .attr('height', function (d) { return height-pad - y(d.N); });
```

Okay, there's plenty going on here, but this code is saying something very simple: for all rectangles (rect) in the graph, load our data, go through it, and for each item append a rect and then define some attributes.

The x scale helps us calculate the horizontal positions and rangeBand gives the width of the bar. The y scale calculates vertical positions and we manually get the height of each bar from y to the bottom. Note that whenever we needed a different value for every element, we defined an attribute as a function (x, y, and height); otherwise, we defined it as a value (width).

Keep this in mind when you're tinkering.

Let's add some flourish and make each bar grow out of the horizontal axis. Time to dip our toes into animations!

Add five lines to the preceding code:

```
svg.selectAll('rect')
  .data(data)
  .enter()
  .append('rect')
```

```
.attr('class', 'bar')
.attr('x', function (d) { return x(d.bucket); })
.attr('width', x.rangeBand())
.attr('y', height-pad)
.transition()
.delay(function (d) { return d.bucket*20; })
.duration(800)
.attr('y', function (d) { return y(d.N); })
.attr('height', function (d) { return height-pad - y(d.N); });
```

The difference is that we statically put all bars at the bottom (`height-pad`) and then entered a transition with `.transition()`. From here on, we define the transition we want.

First, we wanted each bar's transition delayed by 20 milliseconds using `d.bucket*20`. This gives the histogram a neat effect, gradually appearing from left to right instead of jumping up at once. Next, we said we wanted each animation to last just shy of a second with `.duration(800)`. In the end, we defined the final values for the animated attributes—`y` and `height` are the same as in previous code—and d3.js is going to take care of the rest.

Refresh the page and voila! A beautiful histogram appears as shown in the following screenshot:

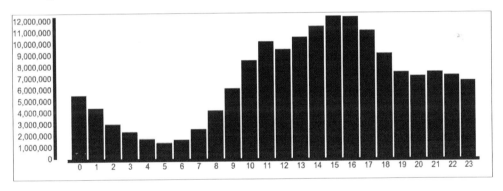

Hmm, not really. We need some CSS to make everything look perfect.

Remember that you can look at the full code on GitHub at `https://github.com/Swizec/d3.js-book-examples/tree/master/ch1` if you didn't get something similar to the preceding screenshot.

Let's go into our HTML file and add some CSS on line 4, right after including bootstrap:

```
<style>
  .axis path,
  .axis line {
    fill: none;
    stroke: #eee;
    shape-rendering: crispEdges;
  }

  .axis text {
    font-size: 11px;
  }

  .bar {
    fill: steelblue;
  }
</style>
```

This is why we added all those classes to shapes. We made the axes thin, gave them a light-gray color, and used a relatively small font for the labels. The bars should be steel blue. Refresh the page now and the histogram is beautiful:

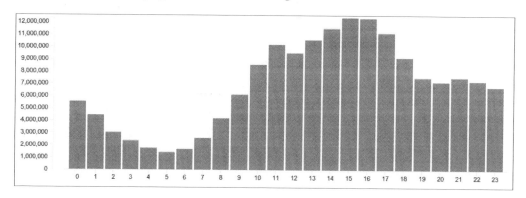

I suggest playing around with the values for `width`, `height`, `left_pad`, and `pad` to get a feel of the power of `d3.js`. You'll notice everything scales and adjusts to any size without having to change the other code. Marvelous!

Summary

We've learned what d3.js is and took a glance at the core philosophy behind how it works. We've also set up a quick and easy environment for prototyping ideas and playing with visualizations. This environment will be assumed throughout the book.

We've also gone through a simple example and created an animated histogram using some of the basics of d3.js. We found out about scales and axes, that the vertical axis is inverted, that any property defined as a function is recalculated for every data point, and that we use a combination of CSS and SVG to make things beautiful.

Most of all, this chapter has given you the basic tools so that you can start playing with d3.js on your own. Tinkering is your friend.

2
A Primer on DOM, SVG, and CSS

In this chapter, we'll take a look at the core technologies that make d3.js tick: the **Document Object Model (DOM)**, **Scalable Vector Graphics (SVG)**, and **Cascading Style Sheets (CSS)**.

You're probably used to manipulating DOM and CSS with libraries such as jQuery or MooTools, but d3.js has a full suite of manipulation tools as well.

SVG is at the core of building truly great visualizations, so we'll take special care to understand it; everything from manually drawing shapes to transformations and path generators.

DOM

The Document Object Model is a language-agnostic model for representing structured documents built in HTML, XML, or similar standards. You can think of it as a tree of nodes that closely resembles the document parsed by the browser.

At the top, there is an implicit document node, which represents the `<html>` tag; browsers create this tag even if you don't specify it and then build the tree off this root node according to what your document looks like. If you have a simple HTML file as follows:

```
<!DOCTYPE html>
<title>A title</title>

<div>
  <p>A paragraph of text</p>
```

```
    </div>

    <ul>
      <li>List item</li>
      <li>List item 2, <em><strong>italic</strong></em></li>
    </ul>
```

Chrome will parse the preceding code to DOM as follows:

In the latest Chrome builds, I can print and play with this in the **Console** tab; you might have to use the **Elements** tab to get the same effect. Moving the cursor over each element will show you where exactly it is placed on the page, which is very handy for debugging.

Manipulating the DOM with d3.js

Every node in a DOM tree comes with a slew of methods and properties that you can use to change the look of the rendered document.

Take for instance the HTML code in our previous example. If we want to change the word `italic` to make it underlined as well as bold and italic (the result of the `<em>` and `<strong>` tags), we would do it using the following code:

```
document.getElementsByTagName('strong')[0].style.setProperty('text-
decoration', 'underline')
```

Wow! What a mouthful.

We took the root `document` node and found every node created from a `<strong>` tag; then we took the first item in this array and added a `text-decoration` property to its `style` property.

The sheer amount of code it took to do something this simple in a document with only eleven nodes is the reason why few people today use the DOM API directly — not to mention all the subtle differences between browsers.

Since we'd like to keep our lives simple and avoid using the DOM directly, we need a library. jQuery is a good choice, but to make things even simpler, we can use d3.js. It comes with everything we need.

That means we can treat HTML as just another type of data visualization. Let that one sink in. HTML is data visualization.

In practice, this means we can use similar techniques to present data as a table or an interactive image. Most of all, we can use the same data.

Let's rewrite the previous example in d3.js:

```
d3.select('strong').style('text-decoration', 'underline')
```

Much simpler! We selected the `strong` element and defined a `style` property. Job done!

By the way, any property you set with d3.js can be dynamic, so you can assign a function as well as a value. This is going to come in handy later.

What we just did is called a **selection**. Since selections are the core of everything we do with d3.js, let's take a closer look.

Selections

A selection is an array of elements pulled from the current document according to a particular CSS selector. Selectors let you apply different functions to the whole selection at once so you never have to loop through the elements manually.

Using CSS selectors to decide which elements to work on gives us a simple language for defining elements in the document. It's actually the same as you're used to from jQuery and CSS itself.

To get the first element with ID as `graph`, we use `.select('#graph')`; to get all the elements with the class `blue`, we write `.selectAll('.blue')`; and to get all the paragraphs in a document, we use `.selectAll('p')`.

We can combine these to get a more complex matching. Think of it as set operations. You can perform an AND operation with ".this.that"; it will get elements with classes this and that. Alternatively, you might perform an OR operation with ".this, .that" to get elements having either the this or that class.

But what if you want to select children elements? Nested selections to the rescue. You can do it with a simple selector such as "tbody td", or you can chain two selectAll calls as .selectAll('tbody').selectAll('td'). Both will select all the cells in a table body. Keep in mind that nested selections maintain the hierarchy of selected elements, which gives us some interesting capabilities. Let's look at a short example.

Selections example

Take the base HTML from our play environment in the first chapter and add a simple table:

```
<table class="table">
  <thead>
    <tr><td>One</td><td>Two</td><td>Three</td><td>Four</td><td>Five</td></tr>
  </thead>
  <tbody>
    <tr><td>q</td><td>w</td><td>e</td><td>r</td><td>t</td></tr>
    <tr><td>a</td><td>s</td><td>d</td><td>f</td><td>g</td></tr>
    <tr><td>z</td><td>x</td><td>c</td><td>v</td><td>b</td></tr>
  </tbody>
</table>
```

Pretty much the standard markup for a table, <thead> and <tbody> define the head and body of the table where each <tr> is a row and each <td> is a cell. Adding the table class tells bootstrap to make the table look pretty for us.

Let's jump into the console and have some fun with selections:

```
d3.selectAll('td').style('color', 'red')
```

The text will promptly turn red. Now let's make everything in the table head bold by chaining two selectAll calls:

```
d3.selectAll('thead').selectAll('td').style('font-weight', 'bold')
```

Great! Let's take nested selections a bit further and make table body cells green in the second and fourth column:

```
d3.selectAll('tbody tr').selectAll('td')
  .style('color', function (d, i) { return i%2 ? 'green' : 'red'; })
```

The two `selectAll` calls gave us all the instances of `td` in the body, separated by rows, giving us an array of three arrays with five elements: `[ Array[5], Array[5], Array[5] ]`. Then we used `style` to change the color of every selected element.

Using a function instead of a static property gave us the fine-grained control we needed. The function is called with a data attribute (we'll discuss more on that later) and an index of the column it's in, that is, the `i` variable. Since we're using nested selections, a third parameter would give us the row. Then we simply return either `'green'` or `'red'` based on the current index.

One thing to keep in mind is that chaining selections can be more efficient than OR selectors when it comes to very large documents. This is because each subsequent selection only searches through the elements matched previously.

Manipulating content

We can do far more than just playing around with selections and changing the properties of the elements. We can manipulate things.

With d3.js, we can change the contents of an element, add new elements, or remove elements we don't want.

Let's add a new column to the table from our previous example:

```
var newCol = d3.selectAll('tr').append('td')
```

We selected all the table rows and then appended a new cell to each using `.append()`. All d3.js actions return the current selection—new cells in this case—so we can chain actions or assign the new selection to a variable (`newCol`) for later use.

We have an empty invisible column on our hands. Let's add some text to spruce things up:

```
newCol.text('a')
```

At least now that it's full of instances of a, we can say a column is present. But that's kind of pointless, so let's follow the pattern set by other columns:

```
newCol.text(function (d, i) { return ['Six', 'y', 'h', 'n'][i] })
```

The trick of dynamically defining the content via a function helps us pick the right string from a list of values depending on the column we're in, which we identify by the index i.

Figured out the pattern yet? Read the top row of the table body.

Similarly, we can remove elements using .remove(). To get rid of the last row in the table, you'd write something as follows:

```
d3.selectAll('tr')[0][3].remove()
```

You have to use [0][3] instead of just [3] because selections are arrays of arrays.

Joining data to selections

We've made it to the fun part of our DOM shenanigans. Remember when I said HTML is data visualization? Joining data to selections is how that happens.

To join data with a selection, we use the .data() function. It takes a data argument in the form of a function or an array, and optionally a function telling d3.js how to differentiate between various parts of the data.

When you join data to a selection, one of the following three things will happen:

- There is more data than was already joined (the length of the data is longer than the length of a selection). You can reference the new entries with the .enter() function.

- There is exactly the same amount of data as before. You can use the selection returned by .data() itself to update element states.

- There is less data than before. You can reference these using the .exit() function.

You can't chain .enter() and .exit() because they are just references and don't create a new selection. This means you will usually want to focus on .enter() and .exit() and handle the three cases separately. Mind you, all three can happen at once.

You must be wondering, "But how's it possible for there to be both more and less data than before?" That's because selection elements are bound to instances of datum, not their number. If you shifted an array and then pushed a new value, the previous first item would go to the .exit() reference and the new addition would go to the .enter() reference.

Let's build something cool with data joins and HTML.

An HTML visualization example

We'll start off with the same HTML file as usual. I'd suggest coding in the `code.js` file from now on because things can get pretty involved. Refresh frequently to keep an eye on what's going on.

Every great visualization needs a dataset; we'll be using the list of all Dr. Who monsters and villains since 1963. It's been published by the *Guardian Datablog* in late December, 2012. You can get the CSV file from `https://github.com/Swizec/d3.js-book-examples/blob/master/ch2/villains.csv`.

We are going to make a table. Not very exciting for sure, but very practical for HTML visualizations.

We begin with a global data variable.

Add the following line at the top of your `code.js` file:

```
var Data;
```

Then we append an empty table to our `graph` div using the following code:

```
var table = d3.select('#graph')
  .append('table')
  .attr('class', 'table');

var thead = table.append('thead'),
  tbody = table.append('tbody');
```

As you can imagine from previous examples, this code selects the target `<div>` tag with ID as `graph` and appends a `table` element with a `class='table'` attribute so that Bootstrap will make it attractive.

The next two lines append empty `thead` and `tbody` elements and assign them to variables for later use.

Now we're going to load our data and assign it to the `Data` variable:

```
var reload = function () {
  d3.csv('villains.csv', function (data) {
    Data = data;
    redraw();
  });
};
reload();
```

We'll be messing with the dataset later, so it's handy to have a function that we can call when we want to reload the data without having to refresh the page.

Because our dataset is in CSV format, we use the `csv` function of d3.js to load and parse it. d3.js is smart enough to understand that the first row in our dataset is not data but a set of labels, so it populates the `data` variable with an array of dictionaries as follows:

```
{
    "Villain": "Abzorbaloff (Victor Kennedy)",
    "Year first": "2006",
    "Year last": "2006",
    "Doc. no.": "10",
    "Doctor actor": "David Tennant",
    "Epi- sodes": "1",
    "Stories, total": "1",
    "Motivation (invasion earth, end of universe, etc)": "Kill humans",
    "Story titles": "Love and Monsters"
}
```

If you run the code right now, Chrome will complain that the `redraw()` function doesn't exist. Let's write one as follows:

```
var redraw = function () {
};
```

We defined a `redraw` variable and assigned an empty function to it.

Our next step is to make this function do something. Let's go into its body (between the two curly braces) and add some code:

```
var tr = tbody.selectAll('tr')
                .data(Data);

    tr.enter()
      .append('tr');

    tr.exit()
      .remove();
```

The code is divided into three parts. The first part selects all the table rows (of which none exist yet) and joins our `Data` using the `.data()` function. The resulting selection is saved in the `tr` variable.

Next we create a table row for every new datum in the dataset using the `.enter()` reference. Right now, that's for all of them.

The last part of this code doesn't do anything yet but will remove any `<tr>` element in the `.exit()` reference once we change the data later.

After execution, the `tr` variable will hold an array of `<tr>` elements, each bound to its respective place in the dataset. The first `<tr>` element holds the first datum, the second holds the second datum, and so on.

Rows are useless without cells. Let's add some by relying on the fact that data stays joined to elements even after a new selection:

```
tr.selectAll('td')
    .data(function (d) { return d3.values(d); })
    .enter()
    .append('td')
    .text(function (d) { return d; });
```

We selected all the `<td>` children of each row (none exist yet). We then had to call the `.data()` function with the same data transformed into a list of values using `d3.values()`. This gave us a new chance to use `.enter()`.

From then on it's more of the same. Each new entry gets its own table cell, and the text is set to the current datum.

Running this code will give you an utterly confusing table specifying all the Dr. Who monsters and villains televised since 1963.

Let's make it clearer. You can write this code at the bottom of the `redraw()` function or right in Chrome's JavaScript console if you want to see some live updating magic.

To sort the table by the villain's first appearance, we write the following code:

```
tbody.selectAll('tr')
    .sort(function (a, b) { return d3.ascending(a['Year first'], b['Year
first']); });
```

Without doing anything else, this code will redraw the table with the new ordering — no refreshing the page, no manually adding or removing elements. Because all our data is joined to the HTML, we didn't even need a reference to the original `tr` selection or the data. Pretty nifty if you ask me.

The `.sort()` function takes only a comparator function. The comparator is given two pieces of data and must decide how to order them: `-1` for being less than b, `0` for being equal, and `1` for being more than b. You can also use `d3.ascending` and `d3.descending` comparators of d3.js.

That's still pretty unclear though. Let's limit our table only to the latest Doctor:

```
Data = Data.filter(function (d) { return d['Doctor actor'] == 'Matt
Smith'; })
redraw()
```

We filtered the dataset so that it only contains rows where the actor is Matt Smith, and then we called the `redraw()` function. The `.exit()` selection does its job and a few hundred rows are removed from the table. Wait… we ended up with a mishmash of actors. Took me a while to figure out what's going on.

JavaScript is a language with instance-based identity, which means that d3.js can't use a `==` b to decide whether two complex objects are the same. Instead, it relies on indexes to identify objects. So when we filtered our data, the first x number of indexes had something in them and were considered unchanged, and the rest were removed. The data already attached to elements doesn't get updated, and we have a bad table on our hands. We can get out of this in two ways.

We could first sort the table and then filter the data as follows:

```
tbody.selectAll('tr').sort(function (a, b) {
    return d3.descending(Number(a['Doc. no.']), Number(b['Doc. no.']));
});
```

As before, we used a comparator to sort; we used a numerical comparison between `a['Doc. no.']` and `b['Doc. no.']` to sort the rows in descending order with the highest number on top.

Running the same code as before will give the desired result:

```
Data = Data.filter(function (d) { return d['Doctor actor'] == 'Matt
Smith'; })
redraw()
```

This worked because Matt Smith was in the first x places of the dataset. But the approach only works for this example. We can use a more robust approach, but it doesn't happen automatically when we change the data. Remember to refresh the page or run `reload()` to get the whole dataset back.

Now we can filter the table directly as follows:

```
tbody.selectAll('tr')
  .filter(function (d) { return d['Doctor actor'] != 'Matt Smith'; })
  .remove()
```

The `.filter()` function takes a single selector as its argument and feeds the current datum to it. When the function returns `false`, the element is removed from the selection; when it returns `true`, the element remains. In the end, we use the `.remove()` function to remove every row we caught. Much more robust, but playing with the data itself is often more elegant. Choose wisely.

SVG

Scalable Vector Graphics is a vector graphics format that describes images with XML. It's been around since 1999 and is supported by all major browsers these days. Unfortunately, Internet Explorer has been a laggard and provides only limited support since Version 9. Vector images can be rendered in any size without becoming fuzzy. This means you can render the same image on a large retina display or a small mobile phone, and it will look great in both cases.

SVG images are made up of shapes you can create from scratch using paths, or put together from basic shapes defined in the standard, for example, a line or a circle. The format itself represents shapes with XML elements and some attributes.

As such, SVG code is just a bunch of text you can edit manually, inspect with your browser's normal debugging tools, and compress with standard text compression algorithms. Being text based also means you can use d3.js to create an image in your browser, then copy and paste the resulting XML to a `.svg` file, and open it with any SVG viewer.

Another consequence is that browsers can consider SVG to be a normal part of the document. You can use CSS for styling, listening for mouse events on specific shapes, and even scripting the image to make animations where images are interactive.

Drawing with SVG

To draw with d3.js, you can add shapes manually by defining the appropriate SVG elements, or you can use helper functions that help you create advanced shapes easily.

Now we're going to go through the very core of what d3.js does. Everything else builds from this, so pay attention.

Let's start by preparing a drawing area in our usual environment. Put this code at the top of a fresh `code.js` file:

```
var svg = d3.select('#graph')
    .append('svg')
    .style('width', 1024)
    .style('height', 768);
```

We appended an `<svg>` element to the main `<div>` tag and adjusted its size. From now on, we'll be using the `svg` variable for drawing.

Manually adding elements and shapes

An SVG image is a collection of elements rendered as shapes and comes with a set of seven basic elements. All but one of these are just an easier way to define a path:

- Text (the only one that isn't a path)
- Straight lines
- Rectangles
- Circles
- Ellipses
- Polylines (a set of straight lines)
- Polygons (a set of straight lines, closing in on itself)

You build SVG images by adding these elements to the canvas and defining some attributes. All of them can have a `stroke` style defining how the edge is rendered, a `fill` style defining how the shape is filled, and all of them can be rotated, skewed, or moved using the `transform` attribute.

Text

Text is the only element that is neither a shape nor does it translate to a path in the background like the others. Let's look at it first so the rest of this chapter can be about shapes:

```
svg.append('text')
  .text("A picture!")
  .attr({x: 10,
    y: 150,
      'text-anchor': 'start'});
```

We took our `svg` element and appended a `text` element. Then we defined its actual text and added some attributes to position the text at the `(x, y)` point and anchored the text at start.

The `text-anchor` attribute defines the horizontal positioning of rendered text in relation to the anchor point defined by `(x, y)`. The positions it understands are the start, the middle, and the end.

We can also fine tune the text's position with an offset defined by the `dx` and `dy` attributes. This is especially handy when adjusting the text margin and baseline relative to the font size because it understands the `em` unit.

Our image looks as follows:

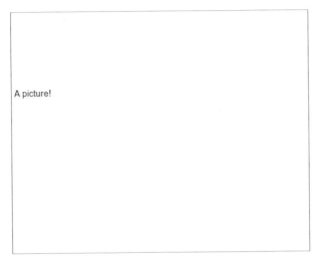

Shapes

Now that text is out of the way, let's look at something useful—shapes, the heart of the rest of this book.

We begin by drawing a straight line using the following code:

```
svg.append('line')
  .attr({x1: 10,
     y1: 10,
     x2: 100,
     y2: 100,
     stroke: 'blue',
     'stroke-width': 3});
```

As before, we took the svg element, appended a line, and defined some attributes. A line is drawn between two points: (x1, y1) and (x2, y2). To make the line visible, we have to define the stroke color and stroke-width attributes as well.

Our line points downwards even though y2 is bigger than y1. Hmm... that's because the origin in most image formats lies in the top-left corner. This means (x=0, y=0) defines the top-left corner of the image.

To draw a rectangle, we can use the rect element:

```
svg.append('rect')
  .attr({x: 200,
    y: 50,
    width: 300,
    height: 400});
```

We appended a rect element to the svg element and defined some attributes. A rectangle is defined by its upper-left corner (x, y), width, and height.

Our image now looks as follows:

We have an unwieldy black rectangle. We can make it prettier by defining three more properties as follows:

```
svg.select('rect')
  .attr({stroke: 'green',
    'stroke-width': 0.5,
    fill: 'white',
    rx: 20,
    ry: 40});
```

This is much better. Our rectangle has a thin, green outline. Rounded corners come from the rx and ry attributes, which define the corner radius along the x and y axis:

Let's try adding a circle:

```
svg.append('circle')
  .attr({cx: 350,
    cy: 250,
    r: 100,
    fill: 'green',
    fill-opacity': 0.5,
    stroke: 'steelblue',
    'stroke-width': 2});
```

A circle is defined by a central point (cx, cy) and a radius r. In this instance, we get a green circle with a steelblue outline in the middle of our rectangle. The fill-opacity attribute tells the circle to be slightly transparent so it doesn't look too strong against the light rectangle:

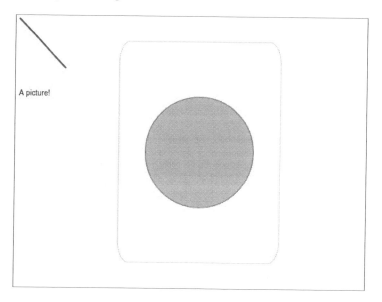

Mathematically speaking, a circle is just a special form of ellipse. By adding another radius and changing the element, we can draw one of these:

```
svg.append('ellipse')
  .attr({cx: 350,
    cy: 250,
    rx: 150,
    ry: 70,
    fill: 'green',
    'fill-opacity': 0.3,
    stroke: 'steelblue',
    'stroke-width': 0.7});
```

We added an `ellipse` element and defined some well-known attributes. The ellipse shape needs a central point (`cx`, `cy`) and two radii, `rx` and `ry`. Setting a low `fill-opacity` attribute makes the circle visible under the ellipse:

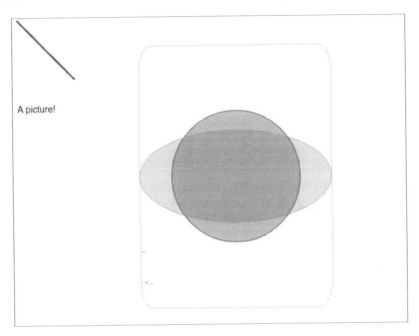

That's nice, but we can make it more interesting using the following code:

```
svg.append('ellipse')
  .attr({cx: 350,
    cy: 250,
    rx: 20,
    ry: 70});
```

The only trick here is that rx is smaller than ry, creating a vertical ellipse. Lovely!

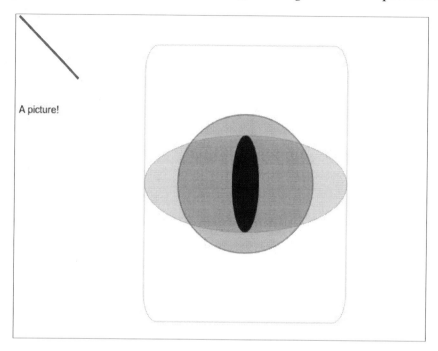

A strange green eye with a random blue line is staring at you, all thanks to manually adding basic SVG elements to the canvas and defining some attributes.

The generated SVG looks in XML form as follows:

```
<svg style="width: 1024px; height: 768px;">
  <text x="10" y="150" text-anchor="start">A picture!</text>
  <line x1="10" y1="10" x2="100" y2="100" stroke="blue" stroke-
width="3"></line>
  <rect x="200" y="50" width="300" height="400" stroke="green" stroke-
width="0.5" fill="white" rx="20" ry="40"></rect>
  <circle cx="350" cy="250" r="100" fill="green" fill-opacity="0.5"
stroke="steelblue" stroke-width="2"></circle>
  <ellipse cx="350" cy="250" rx="150" ry="70" fill="green" fill-
opacity="0.3" stroke="steelblue" stroke-width="0.7"></ellipse>
  <ellipse cx="350" cy="250" rx="20" ry="70"></ellipse>
</svg>
```

Yeah, I wouldn't want to write that by hand either.

But you can see all the elements and attributes we added before. Being able to look at an image file and understand what's going on might come in handy some day. It's certainly cool. Usually when you open an image in a text editor, all you get is binary gobbledygook.

Now, I know I mentioned earlier that polylines and polygons are also basic SVG elements. The only reason I'm leaving off the explanation of these basic elements is because with d3.js, we have some great tools to work with them. Trust me, you don't want to do them manually.

Transformations

Before jumping onto more complicated things, we have to look at transformations.

Without going into too much mathematical detail, it suffices to say that transformations, as used in SVG, are affine transformations of coordinate systems used by shapes in our drawing. The beautiful thing is they can be defined as matrix multiplications, making them very efficient to compute.

But, unless your brain is made out of linear algebra, using transformations as matrices can get very tricky. SVG helps out by coming with a set of predefined transformations, namely, `translate()`, `scale()`, `rotate()`, `skewX()`, and `skewY()`.

According to Wikipedia, an affine transformation is any transformation that preserves points, straight lines, and planes, while keeping sets of parallel lines parallel. They don't necessarily preserve distances but do preserve ratios of distances between points on a straight line. This means if you take a rectangle, you can use affine transformations to rotate it, make it bigger, and even turn it into a parallelogram; however, no matter what you do, it will never become a trapezoid.

Computers handle transformations as matrix multiplication because any sequence of transformations can be collapsed into a single matrix. This means they only have to apply a single transformation that encompasses your sequence of transformations when drawing the shape, which is handy.

We will apply transformations with the `transform` attribute. We can define multiple transformations that are applied in order. The order of operations can change the result. You'll notice this in the following examples.

Let's move our eye to the edge of the rectangle:

```
svg.selectAll('ellipse, circle')
    .attr('transform', 'translate(150, 0)');
```

We selected everything our eye is made of (two ellipses and a circle), and then applied the `translate` transformation. It moved the shape's origin along the `(150, 0)` vector, moving the shape 150 pixels to the right and 0 pixels down.

If you try moving it again, you'll notice new transformations are applied according to the original state of our shape. That's because there can only be one `transform` attribute per shape.

Our picture looks as follows:

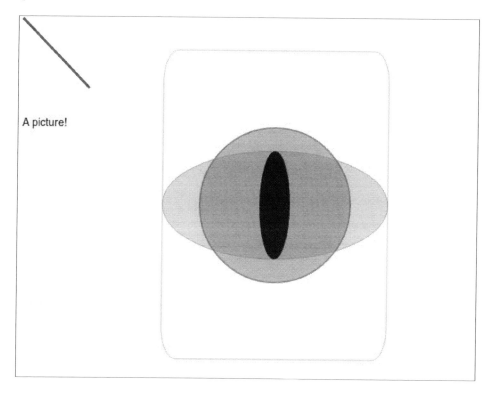

Let's rotate the eye by 45 degrees:

```
svg.selectAll('ellipse, circle')
    .attr('transform', 'translate(150, 0) rotate(45)');
```

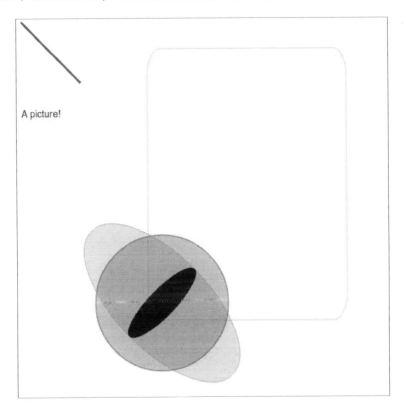

That's not what we wanted at all.

What tricked us is that rotations happen around the origin of the image, not the shape. We have to define the rotation axis ourselves:

```
svg.selectAll('ellipse, circle')
    .attr('transform', 'translate(150, 0) rotate(-45, 350, 250)');
```

By adding two more arguments to `rotate()`, we defined the rotation axis and achieved the desired result:

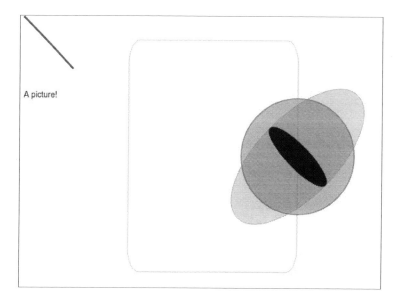

Let's make the eye a little bigger with the `scale()` transformation:

```
svg.selectAll('ellipse, circle')
   .attr('transform', 'translate(150, 0) rotate(-45, 350, 250)
scale(1.2)');
```

This will make our object `1.2` times bigger along both the axes; two arguments would have scaled by different factors along the x and y axes:

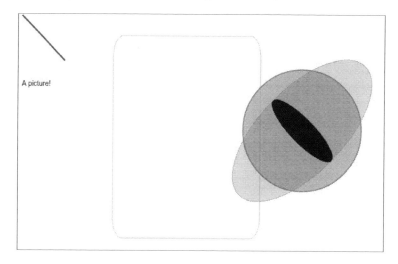

Once again, we pushed the position of the eye because scaling is anchored at the zeroth point of the whole image. We have to use another `translate` to move it back. But the coordinate system we're working on is now rotated by 45 degrees and scaled. This makes things tricky. We need to translate between the two coordinate systems to move the eye correctly. To move the eye 70 pixels to the left, we have to move it along each axis by *70*sqrt(2)/2* pixels, which is the result of cosine and sine at an angle of 45.

But that's just messy. The number looks funny, and we worked way too much for something so simple. Let's change the order of operations instead:

```
svg.selectAll('ellipse, circle')
  .attr('transform', 'translate(150, 0) scale(1.2) translate(-70, 0)
rotate(-45, '+(350/1.2)+', '+(250/1.2)+')');
```

Much better! We get exactly what we wanted:

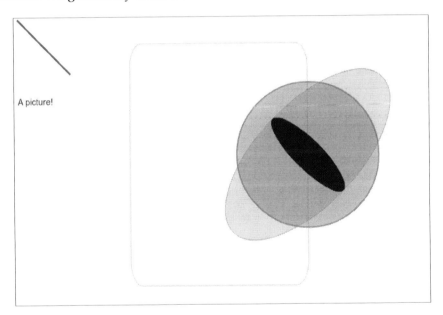

A picture!

A lot has changed, let's take a look.

First we translate to our familiar position and then scale by `1.2`, pushing the eye out of position. We fix this by translating back to the left by `70` pixels and then finally performing the `45` degree rotation, making sure to divide the pivot point by `1.2`.

There's one more thing we can do to the poor eye; skew it. Two skew transformations exist: skewX and skewY. Both skew along their respective axis:

```
svg.selectAll('ellipse, circle')
  .attr('transform', 'translate(150, 0) scale(1.2) translate(-70, 0)
rotate(-45, '+(350/1.2)+', '+(250/1.2)+') skewY(20)');
```

We just bolted skewY(20) on to the end of the transform attribute.

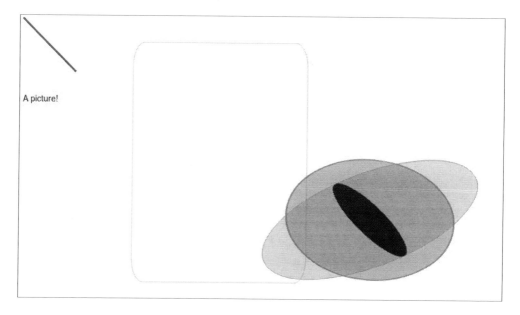

We have once more destroyed our careful centering. Fixing this is left as an exercise for the reader (I've always wanted to say that).

All said, transformations really are just matrix multiplication. In fact, you can define any transformation you want with the matrix() function. I suggest taking a look at exactly what kind of matrix produces each of the preceding effects. The W3C specification available at http://www.w3.org/TR/SVG/coords. html#EstablishingANewUserSpace can help.

Using paths

Path elements define outlines of shapes that can be filled, stroked, and so on. They are generalizations of all other shapes and can be used to draw nearly anything.

Most of the path's magic stems from the d attribute; it uses a mini language of three basic commands:

- M, meaning moveto
- L, meaning lineto
- Z, meaning closepath

To create a rectangle, we might write something as follows:

```
svg.append('path')
    .attr({d: 'M 100 100 L 300 100 L 200 300 z',
        stroke: 'black',
        'stroke-width': 2,
        fill: 'red',
        'fill-opacity': 0.7});
```

We appended a new element to our svg and then defined some attributes. The interesting bit is the d attribute, M 100 100 L 300 100 L 200 300 z. Breaking this down, you can see we first moved to (100, 100), drew a line on (300, 100), another line on (200, 300), and then closed the path.

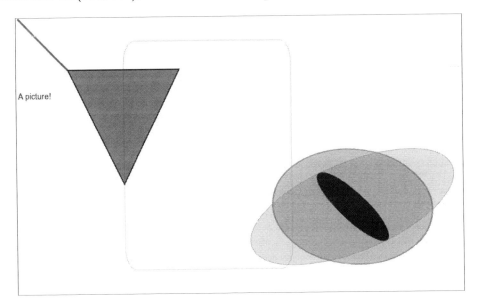

The power of paths doesn't stop there, though. Commands beyond the M, L, Z combination give us tools to create curves and arcs. But creating complex shapes by hand is beyond tediousness.

d3.js comes with some helpful path generator functions that take JavaScript and turn it into path definitions. We'll be looking at those next.

Our image is getting pretty crowded, so let's restart the environment.

To start things off, we'll draw the humble sine function. Once again, we begin by preparing the drawing area:

```
var width = 1024,
  height = 768,
  margin = 10;

var svg = d3.select('#graph')
  .append('svg')
  .attr('width', width+2*margin)
  .attr('height', height+2*margin);

var g = svg.append('g')
  .attr('transform', 'translate('+margin+', '+margin+')');
```

We appended an `svg` element to our `#graph` div and set a large enough `width` and `height` for our evil plans. Then, we appended a `g` element to put our chart in. The `g` element is a logical grouping of SVG shapes, improving the semantics of our document and making it easier to use.

Next, we need some data, which is the `sine` function.

```
var sine = d3.range(0,10).map(
  function (k) { return [0.5*k*Math.PI,
                         Math.sin(0.5*k*Math.PI)]; });
```

Using `d3.range(0,10)` gives us a list of integers from zero to nine. We map over them and turn each into a tuple, actually a 2-length array representing the maxima, minima, and zeroes of the curve. You might remember from your math class that sine starts at (0,0), then goes to (Pi/2, 1), (Pi, 0), (3Pi/2, -1), and so on.

We'll feed these as data into a path generator.

Path generators are really the meat of d3.js's magic. We'll discuss the gravy of the magic in *Chapter 5, Layouts – d3's Black Magic*. They are essentially a function that takes some data (joined to elements) and produces a path definition in SVG's path mini language. All path generators can be told how to use our data. We also get to play with the final output a great deal.

Line

To create a line we use the `d3.svg.line()` generator and define the x- and y-accessor functions. Accessors tell the generator how to read the x and y coordinates from datapoints.

We begin by defining two scales. Scales are functions that map from a domain to a range; we'll talk more about them in the next chapter:

```
var x = d3.scale.linear()
    .range([0, width/2-margin])
    .domain(d3.extent(sine, function (d) { return d[0]; })),
  y = d3.scale.linear().range([height/2-margin, 0]).domain([-1, 1]);
```

Now we get to define a simple path generator:

```
var line = d3.svg.line()
    .x(function (d) { return x(d[0]); })
      .y(function (d) { return y(d[1]); });
```

It is just a matter of taking the basic line generator and attaching some accessors to it. We told the generator to use our x scale on the first element and the y scale on the second element of every tuple. By default, it assumes our dataset as a collection of arrays defining points directly so that `d[0]` is x and `d[1]` is y.

All that's left now is drawing the actual line:

```
g.append('path')
  .datum(sine)
  .attr("d", line)
  .attr({stroke: 'steelblue',
       'stroke-width': 2,
         fill: 'none'});
```

Append a path, and add the `sine` data using `.datum()`. Using this instead of `.data()` means we can render the function as a single element instead of creating a new line for every point. We let our generator define the d attribute. The rest just makes things visible.

Our graph looks as follows:

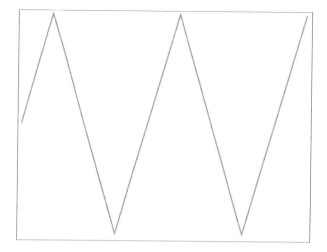

If you look at the generated code, you'll see this sort of gobbledygook:

```
d="M0,192L56.88888888888889,0L113.77777777777779,191.99999999999994L17
0.66666666666669,384L227.55555555555557,192.00000000000006L284.4444444
4444446,0L341.33333333333337,191.99999999999991L398.2222222222223,384L
455.11111111111114,192.00000000000009L512,0"
```

See! I told you nobody wants to write that by hand.

That's a very jagged `sine` function we've got there, nothing similar to what the math teacher used to draw in high school. We can make it better with interpolation.

Interpolation is the act of guessing where unspecified points of a line should appear, considering the points we do know. By default, we're using the `linear` interpolator that just draws straight lines between points.

Let's try something else:

```
g.append('path')
  .datum(sine)
  .attr("d", line.interpolate('step-before'))
  .attr({stroke: 'black',
    'stroke-width': 1,
    fill: 'none'});
```

It is the same code as before, but we used the `step-before` interpolator and changed the styling to produce this:

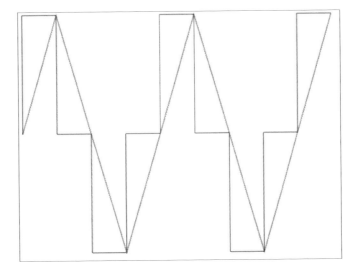

d3.js offers 12 line interpolators in total, which I am not going to list here. You can look them up on the official wiki page at https://github.com/mbostock/d3/wiki/SVG-Shapes#wiki-line_interpolate.

I suggest trying out all of them to get a feel of what they do.

Area

An area is the colored part between two lines, a polygon really.

We define an area similar to how we define a line, so take a path generator and tell it how to use our data. For a simple horizontal area, we have to define one x accessor and two y accessors, y0 and y1, for both the bottom and the top.

We'll compare different generators side by side, so let's add a new graph:

```
var g2 = svg.append('g')
    .attr('transform', 'translate('+(width/2+margin)+', '+margin+')');
```

Now we define an `area` generator and draw an area.

```
var area = d3.svg.area()
    .x(function (d) { return x(d[0]); })
    .y0(height/2)
```

```
      .y1(function (d) { return y(d[1]); })
      .interpolate('basis');

  g2.append('path')
    .datum(sine)
    .attr("d", area)
    .attr({fill: 'steelblue',
      'fill-opacity': 0.4});
```

We took a vanilla `d3.svg.area()` path generator and told it to get the coordinates through the x and y scales we defined earlier. The `basis` interpolator will use a B-spline to create a smooth curve from our data.

To draw the bottom edge, we defined `y0` as the bottom of our graph and produced a colored sine approximation:

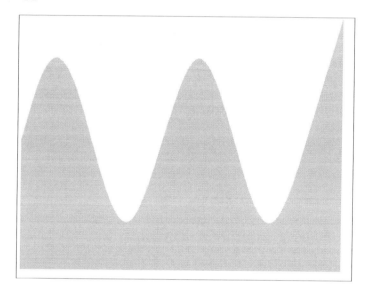

Areas are often used together with lines that make an important edge stand out. Let's try that:

```
  g2.append('path')
    .datum(sine)
    .attr("d", line.interpolate('basis'))
    .attr({stroke: 'steelblue',
      'stroke-width': 2,
      fill: 'none'});
```

We could re-use the same line generator as before; we just need to make sure that we use the same interpolator as for the area. This way, the image looks much better:

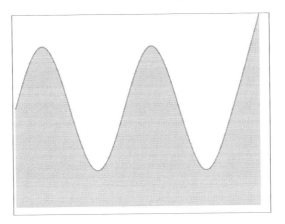

Arc

An arc is a circular path with an inner and outer radius, going from one angle to another. They are often used for pie and donut charts.

Everything works as before; we just tell the base generator how to use our data. The only difference is that this time the default accessors expect named attributes instead of 2-value arrays we've gotten used to.

Let's draw an arc:

```
var arc = d3.svg.arc();

var g3 = svg.append('g')
        .attr('transform', 'translate('+margin+',
'+(height/2+margin)+')');

g3.append('path')
  .attr("d", arc({outerRadius: 100,
    innerRadius: 50,
    startAngle: -Math.PI*0.25,
    endAngle: Math.PI*0.25}))
  .attr('transform', 'translate(150, 150)')
  .attr('fill', 'lightslategrey');
```

This time we could get away with using the default d3.svg.arc() generator. Instead of using data, we calculated the angles by hand and also nudged the arc towards the center.

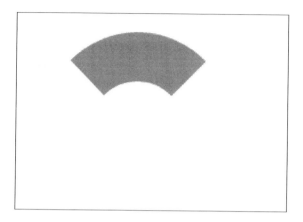

See, a simple arc. Rejoice!

Even though SVG normally uses degrees, the start and end angles use radians. The zero angle points upwards with negative values going anticlockwise and positive values going the other way. Every *2Pi* we come back to zero.

Symbol

Sometimes when visualizing data, we need a simple way to mark datapoints. That's where symbols come in, tiny glyphs used to distinguish between datapoints.

The d3.svg.symbol() generator takes a type accessor and a size accessor, and leaves the positioning to us. We are going to add some symbols to our area chart showing where the function is going when it crosses zero.

As always, we start with a path generator:

```
var symbols = d3.svg.symbol()
    .type(function (d, i) {
      if (d[1] > 0) {
        return 'triangle-down';
      }else{
        return 'triangle-up';
      }
    })
    .size(function (d, i) {
      if (i%2) {
        return 0;
```

```
    }else{
      return 64;
    }
  });
```

We've given the d3.svg.symbol() generator a type accessor telling it to draw a downward pointing triangle when the y coordinate is positive and an upward one when not positive. This works because our sine data isn't mathematically perfect due to Math.PI not being infinite and due to floating point precision; we get infinitesimal numbers close to zero whose signedness depends on whether the Math.sin argument is slightly less or slightly more than the perfect point for sin=0.

The size accessor tells symbol() how much area each symbol should occupy. Because every other datapoint is close to zero, we hide the others with an area equal to zero.

Now we can draw some symbols:

```
g2.selectAll('path')
  .data(sine)
  .enter()
  .append('path')
  .attr('d', symbols)
  .attr('transform', function (d) { return 'translate('+x(d[0])+','+y
(d[1])+')'; })
  .attr({stroke: 'steelblue',
       'stroke-width': 2,
       fill: 'white'});
```

Go through the data, append a new path for each entry, and turn it into a symbol moved into position. The result looks as follows:

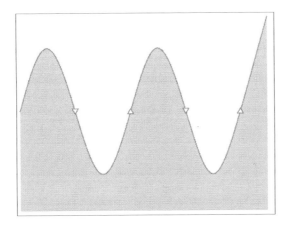

You can see other available symbols by printing d3.svg.symbolTypes.

Chord

Good news! We are leaving the world of simple charts and entering the world of magic.

Chords are most often used to display relations between group elements when arranged in a circle. They use quadratic Bezier curves to create a closed shape connecting two points on an arc.

If you don't have a strong background in computer graphics, that tells you nothing. A basic chord looks similar to half a villain's moustache:

To draw that, we use the following piece of code:

```
g3.append('g').selectAll('path')
  .data([{
    source: {radius: 50,
             startAngle: -Math.PI*0.30,
             endAngle: -Math.PI*0.20},
    target: {radius: 50,
             startAngle: Math.PI*0.30,
             endAngle: Math.PI*0.30}}])
  .enter()
  .append('path')
  .attr("d", d3.svg.chord());
```

This code adds a new grouping element, defines a dataset with a single datum, and appends a path using the default d3.svg.chord() generator for the d attribute.

The data itself plays right into the hands of the default accessors. Source defines where the chord begins and target where it ends. Both are fed to another set of accessors, specifying the arc's radius, startAngle, and endAngle. As with the arc generator, angles are defined using radians.

Let's make up some data and draw a chord diagram:

```
var data = d3.zip(d3.range(0, 12),
                            d3.shuffle(d3.range(0, 12))),
    colors = ['linen', 'lightsteelblue', 'lightcyan',
                   'lavender', 'honeydew', 'gainsboro'];
```

Nothing too fancy. We defined two arrays of numbers, shuffled one, and merged them into an array of pairs; we will look at the details in the next chapter. Then we defined some colors.

```
var chord = d3.svg.chord()
    .source(function (d) { return d[0]; })
    .target(function (d) { return d[1]; })
    .radius(150)
    .startAngle(function (d) { return -2*Math.PI*(1/data.length)*d; })
    .endAngle(function (d) {
        return -2*Math.PI*(1/data.length)*((d-1)%data.length); });
```

All of this just defines the generator. We're going to divide a circle into sections and connect random pairs with chords.

The `.source()` and `.target()` accessors tell us the first item in every pair is the source and the second is the target. For `startAngle`, we remember a full circle is *2Pi* and divide it by the number of sections. Finally, to pick a section, we multiply by the current datum. The `endAngle` accessor is more of the same, except with datums offset by one.

```
g3.append('g')
    .attr('transform', 'translate(300, 200)')
    .selectAll('path')
    .data(data)
    .enter()
    .append('path')
    .attr('d', chord)
    .attr('fill', function (d, i) { return colors[i%colors.length]; })
    .attr('stroke', function (d, i) { return colors[(i+1)%colors.
length]; });
```

To draw the actual diagram we create a new grouping, join the dataset, and then append a path for each datum. The `chord` generator gives it a shape. To make everything look better, we define colors dynamically with the `colors` array.

The end result changes with every refresh but looks something like this:

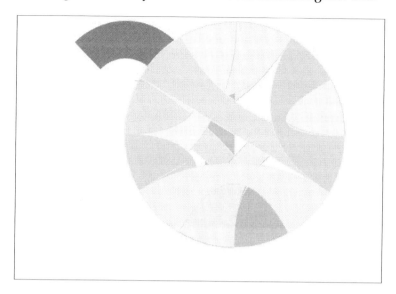

Diagonal

The `diagonal` generator creates cubic Bezier curves—smooth curves between two points. It is very useful for visualizing trees with a node-link diagram.

Once again, the default accessors assume your data is a dictionary with keys named after the specific accessor. You need `source` and `target`, which are fed into `projection`, which then projects Cartesian coordinates into whatever coordinate space you like. By default, it just returns Cartesian coordinates.

Let's draw a moustache. Trees are hard without `d3.layouts` and we'll do those later:

```
var g4 = svg.append('g')
    .attr('transform', 'translate('+(width/2)+','+(height/2)+')');

var moustache = [
  {source: {x: 250, y: 100}, target: {x: 500, y: 90}},
  {source: {x: 500, y: 90}, target: {x: 250, y: 120}},
  {source: {x: 250, y: 120}, target: {x: 0, y: 90}},
  {source: {x: 0, y: 90}, target: {x: 250, y: 100}},
  {source: {x: 500, y: 90}, target: {x: 490, y: 80}},
  {source: {x: 0, y: 90}, target: {x: 10, y: 80}}
];
```

We started off with a fresh graph on our drawing area and defined some data that should create a sweet 'stache:

```
g4.selectAll('path')
  .data(moustache)
  .enter()
  .append('path')
  .attr("d", d3.svg.diagonal())
  .attr({stroke: 'black',
             fill: 'none'});
```

The rest is a simple matter of joining data to our drawing and using the `d3.svg.diagonal()` generator for the `d` attribute:

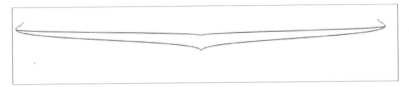

Okay, it's a bit Daliesque. It may be, but it doesn't really look anything like a moustache. That's because the tangents defining how Bezier curves bend are tweaked to create good-looking fan-out in tree diagrams. Unfortunately d3.js doesn't give us a simple way of changing these, and manually defining Bezier curves through SVG's path mini language is tedious at best.

Either way, we have created a side-by-side comparison of path generators:

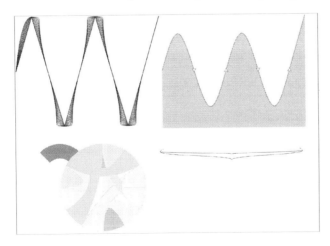

Axes

But we haven't done anything useful with our paths and shapes yet. One way we can do that is using lines and text to create graph axes. It would be tedious though, so d3.js makes our lives easier with axis generators. They take care of drawing a line, putting on some ticks, adding labels, evenly spacing them, and so on.

A d3.js axis is just a combination of path generators configured for awesomeness. All we have to do for a simple linear axis is create a scale and tell the axis to use it. That's it!

For a more customized axis, we might have to define the desired number of ticks and specify the labels, perhaps something even more interesting. There are even ways to make circular axes.

Using a fresh version of the environment, let's create an axis.

We begin with a drawing area:

```
var width = 800,
height = 600,
margin = 20,
svg = d3.select('#graph')
   .append('svg')
   .attr({width: width,
                height: height});
```

We also need a linear scale:

```
var x = d3.scale.linear().domain([0, 100]).range([margin, width-margin]);
```

Our axis is going to use the following to translate data points (domain) to coordinates (range):

```
var axis = d3.svg.axis()
     .scale(x);
var a = svg.append('g')
   .attr('transform', 'translate(0, 30)')
   .data(d3.range(0, 100))
   .call(axis);
```

We've told the `d3.svg.axis()` generator to use our x scale. Then, we simply created a new grouping element, joined some data, and called the axis. It's very important to call the `axis` generator on all of the data at once so it can handle appending its own element.

The result doesn't look good at all.

Axes are complex objects, so fixing this problem is convoluted without CSS, which comes in the next section.

For now, adding this code will be sufficient:

```
a.selectAll('path')
  .attr({fill: 'none',
      stroke: 'black',
      'stroke-width': 0.5});
a.selectAll('line')
  .attr({fill: 'none',
      stroke: 'black',
      'stroke-width': 0.3});
```

An axis is a collection of paths and lines; we give them some swagger and get a nice-looking axis in return:

If you play around with the amount, make sure the scale's domain and the range's max value match, and you'll notice axes are smart enough to always pick the perfect amount of ticks.

Let's compare what the different settings do to axes. We're going to loop through several axes and render the same data.

Wrap your axis-drawing code in a loop by adding this line just above `svg.append('g')`. Don't forget to close off the loop just after the last `stroke-width`:

```
axes.forEach(function (axis, i) {
```

You should also change the `.attr('transform', ...)` line to put each axis 50 pixels below the previous one.

```
.attr('transform', 'translate(0, '+(i*50+margin)+')')
```

Now that's done, we can start defining an array of axes:

```
var axes = [
  d3.svg.axis().scale(x),

  d3.svg.axis().scale(x)
    .ticks(5)
];
```

Two for now: one is the plain vanilla version and the other will render with exactly 5 ticks:

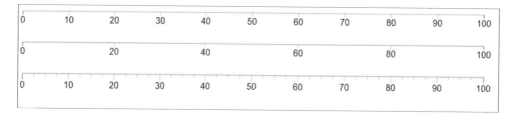

It worked! The `axis` generator figured out which ticks are best left off and relabeled everything without us doing much.

Let's add more axes to the array and see what happens:

```
d3.svg.axis().scale(x)
  .tickSubdivide(3)
  .tickSize(10, 5, 10)
```

With `.tickSubdivide()`, we instruct the generator to add some subdivisions between the major ticks; `.tickSize()` tells it to make the minor ticks smaller. The arguments are major, minor, and end tick size:

For our final trick, let's define some custom ticks and place them above the axis. We'll add another axis to the array:

```
d3.svg.axis().scale(x)
   .tickValues([0, 20, 50, 70, 100])
   .tickFormat(function (d, i) {
      return ['a', 'e', 'i', 'o', 'u'][i];
   })
   .orient('top')
```

Three things happen here: `.tickValues()` exactly defines which values should have a tick, `.tickFormat()` specifies how to render the labels — d3 comes with a slew of helpful formatters in `d3.format` by the way — and finally `.orient('top')` puts the labels above their axis.

You might have guessed the default orient is `'bottom'`. For a vertical axis, you can use `'left'` or `'right'` but don't forget to assign an appropriate scale.

CSS

Cascading Stylesheets have been with us since 1996, making them one of the oldest staples of the Web, even though they only reached widespread popularity with the tables versus CSS wars of the early 2000s.

You're probably familiar with using CSS for styling HTML. So this section will be a refreshing breeze after all that SVG stuff.

My favorite thing about CSS is its simplicity; refer to the following code.

```
selector {
     attribute: value;
}
```

And that's it. Everything you need to know about CSS in three lines.

The selectors can get fairly complicated and are beyond the scope of this book. I suggest looking around the Internet for a good guide. We just need to know some basics:

- `path`: Selects all the `<path>` elements
- `.axis`: Selects all the elements with a `class="axis"` attribute
- `.axis line`: Selects all the `<line>` elements that are children of `class="axis"` elements
- `.axis, line`: Selects all the `class="axis"` and `<line>` elements

Right now you might be thinking, "Oh hey! That's the same as selectors for d3.js selections." Yes! It is exactly the same. d3.js selections are a subset of CSS selectors.

We can invoke CSS with d3.js in three ways: define a class attribute with the `.attr()` method, which can be brittle; use the `.classed()` method, the preferred way to define classes; or define styling directly with the `.style()` method.

Let's improve the axes example from before and make the styling less cumbersome.

Go into the HTML and add some CSS right before the `<div id="graph">` tag as follows:

```
<style>
  .axis path,
  .axis line {
    fill: none;
    stroke: black;
    stroke-width: 1px;
    shape-rendering: crispEdges;
  }

  .axis text {
    font-size: 11px;
  }

  .axis.red line,
  .axis.red path {
    stroke: red;
  }
</style>
```

It is very similar to changing SVG attributes directly, but with CSS. We used `stroke` and `fill` to define the shape of the line and set `shape-rendering` to `crispEdges`. This will make things better.

We've also defined an extra type of axis with red lines.

Now we fix the drawing loop to look as follows:

```
axes.forEach(function (axis, i) {
  var a = svg.append('g')
        .classed('axis', true)
        .classed('red', i%2 == 0)
        .attr('transform', 'translate(0, '+(i*50+margin)+')')
        .data(d3.range(0, 100))
        .call(axis);
});
```

None of that foolishness with specifying the same looks five times in a row. Using the `.classed()` function, we add the `axis` class to each axis and every second axis is red. `.classed()` adds the specified class if the second argument is true and removes it otherwise.

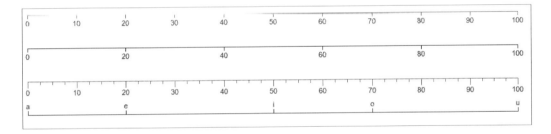

Colors

Beautiful visualizations often involve color beyond the basic names you can think of off the top of your head. Sometimes you want to play with colors depending on what the data looks like.

d3.js has us covered with a slew of functions devoted to manipulating color in four popular color spaces: RGB, HSL, HCL, and L*a*b. The most useful for us are going to be RGB (red green blue) and HSL (hue saturation lightness), which is secretly just another way of looking at RGB. Either way, all color spaces use the same functions, so you can use what fits your needs best.

To construct an RGB color, we use d3.rgb(r, g, b) where r, g, and b specify the channel values for red, green, and blue. We can also replace the triplet with a simple CSS color argument. Then we get to make the color darker or brighter, which is much better than shading by hand.

Time to play with color in a fresh environment. We'll draw two color wheels with their brightness changing from the center towards the outside.

As always, we begin with some variables and a drawing area:

```
var width = 1024,
    height = 768,
    rings = 15;

var svg = d3.select('#graph')
        .append('svg')
        .style({width: width,
                height: height});
```

The main variable henceforth will be rings; it will tell the code how many levels of brightness we want. We also need some basic colors and a way to calculate angles:

```
var colors = d3.scale.category20b();
var angle = d3.scale.linear().domain([0, 20]).range([0, 2*Math.PI]);
```

colors is technically a scale, but we'll use it as data. Category20b is one of four predefined color scales that come with d3.js—an easy way to get a list of well picked colors.

To calculate angles, we're using a linear scale that maps the [0, 20] domain to a full circle [0, 2*pi].

Next we need an arc generator and two data accessors to change the color shade for every ring:

```
var arc = d3.svg.arc()
    .innerRadius(function (d) { return d*50/rings; })
    .outerRadius(function (d) { return 50+d*50/rings; })
    .startAngle(function (d, i, j) { return angle(j); })
    .endAngle(function (d, i, j) { return angle(j+1); });

var shade = {
  darker: function (d, j) { return d3.rgb(colors(j)).darker(d/rings);
},
  brighter: function (d, j) { return d3.rgb(colors(j)).brighter(d/
rings); }
};
```

The arc will calculate the inner and outer radii from a simple ring counter, and the angles will use the `angle` scale, which will automatically calculate the correct radian values. The `j` argument tells us which arc section is currently being drawn.

Since we're making two pictures, we can simplify the code by using two different shaders from a dictionary.

Each shader will take a `d3.rgb()` color from the colors scale and then darken or brighten it by the appropriate number of steps, depending on which ring it's drawing. Once again, the `j` argument tells us which arc section we're in, and the `d` argument tells us which ring we're at.

Finally, we draw the two color wheels:

```
[[100, 100, shade.darker],
 [300, 100, shade.brighter]].forEach(function (conf) {
  svg.append('g')
    .attr('transform', 'translate('+conf[0]+', '+conf[1]+')')
    .selectAll('g')
    .data(colors.range())
    .enter()
    .append('g')
    .selectAll('path')
    .data(function (d) { return d3.range(0, rings); })
    .enter()
    .append('path')
    .attr("d", arc)
    .attr('fill', function (d, i, j) { return conf[2](d, j); });
});
```

Wow! That's quite a bit of code.

We take two triplets, each defining the color wheel's position and which shader to use; then call a function that draws a shiny colorful circle with each.

For each circle, we append a `<g>` element and move it into position, and then use `colors.range()` to get a full list of colors and join it as data. For every new color, we create another `<g>` element and select all the `<path>` elements it contains.

Here things get magical. We join more data but just an array of numbers going from 0 to `rings` this time. For every element in this array, we append a `<path>` element and use the `arc` generator to define its shape. Finally we calculate the `fill` attribute with an appropriately shaded color.

The result looks as follows:

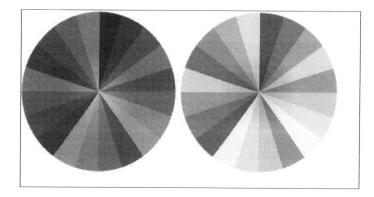

Our main trick was that joining a second dimension of data retains the knowledge of the first dimension via the third attribute supplied to data accessors.

Summary

Wow! We've gone through so much in this chapter.

You should now have a firm grasp of the basics that go into great visualizations. We've gone through DOM manipulation and looked at SVG in great detail, everything from drawing shapes manually to path generators. Finally we looked at CSS as a better alternative for making things pretty.

Everything we look at from now on is going to build on these basics, but you now have the tools to draw anything you can think of. The rest of this book just shows you more elegant ways of doing it.

3
Making Data Useful

At its core, d3.js is a data manipulation library. We're going to take a look at making our datasets useful with both d3.js and plain old JavaScript.

We start with a quick dip into functional programming to bring everyone up to speed. You can skip this part if you use Haskell, Scala, or Lisp, or already write JavaScript in a functional style.

We continue loading external data, taking a closer look at the scales I can't stop writing about, and finish with some temporal and geographic data.

Thinking about data functionally

Due to the functional design of d3.js, we have to start thinking of our code and data with a functional mindset.

The good news is that JavaScript almost counts as a functional language; there are enough features to get the benefits of a functional style, and also provides enough freedom to do things imperatively or in an object-oriented way. The bad news is that, unlike real functional languages, the environment gives no guarantee about our code.

In this section, we'll go through the basics of functional-style coding and look at wrangling the data so that it's easier to work with. If you want to try proper functional programming, I suggest looking at Haskell and *Learn You a Haskell for Great Good* available at `http://learnyouahaskell.com/`.

The idea behind functional programming is simple — compute by relying only on function arguments. Simple, but the consequences are far reaching.

The biggest consequence is that we don't have to rely on state, which in turn gives us referential transparency. This means functions executed with the same parameters will always give the same results regardless of when or how they're called.

In practice this means we design the code and dataflow, that is, get data as input, execute a sequence of functions that pass changed data down the chain, and eventually get a result.

You've already seen this in previous examples.

Our dataset started and ended as an array of values. We performed some actions for each item and we relied only on the current item when deciding what to do. We also had the current index, so we could cheat a little with an imperative approach by looking ahead and behind in the stream.

Built-in array functions

JavaScript comes with a slew of array-manipulation functions. We'll focus on those which are more functional in nature, the iteration methods.

A smart man once told me you can model any algorithm by using map and reduce. But he was wrong. What you need is recursion, a way to add two arrays together, the ability to get the first and second element of an array, an equality comparator, and a way to decide if something is a value or an array. In fact that's how LISP is defined.

But you will get pretty far with map, reduce, and filter in combination with their predicates.

The map command applies a function on every element of an array and returns a new array with changed values:

```
> [1,2,3,4].map(function (d) { return d+1; })
[ 2, 3, 4, 5 ]
```

The reduce function uses a combining function and a starting value to collapse an array into a single value:

```
> [1,2,3,4].reduce(function (accumulator, current) { return
accumulator+current; }, 0)
10
```

The filter function goes through an array and keeps elements for which the predicate returns true:

```
> [1,2,3,4].filter(function (d) { return d%2; })
[ 1, 3 ]
```

Two more useful functions are `.every()` and `.some()`, which are true if every or some items in the array are true. Sometimes, using `.forEach()` instead of `.map()` is better because `forEach` operates on the original array instead of creating a copy, which is important for working with large arrays and is mainly used for the side-effect.

These functions are relatively new to JavaScript, whereas `map` and `filter` have existed since JavaScript 1.7, and `reduce` since 1.8; these are also a part of the emerging ECMAScript 6 standard and, thus, not supported on older browsers. You can use libraries, such as underscore.js or one of the various es6 shims to support older browsers.

Data functions of d3.js

d3.js comes with plenty of its own array functions. They mostly have to do with handling data; it comprises calculating averages, ordering, bisecting arrays, and many helper functions for associative arrays.

Let's play with data functions and draw an unsolved mathematical problem named Ulam spiral. Discovered in 1963, it reveals patterns in the distribution of prime numbers on a two-dimensional plane. So far, nobody has found a formula that explains them.

We'll construct the spiral by simulating Ulam's pen-and-paper method; we'll write natural numbers in a spiraling pattern, and then remove all non-primes.

Instead of numbers we'll draw dots. The first stage in our experiment will look as follows:

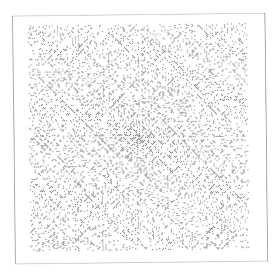

Doesn't look like much, but that's only the first 5,000 primes in a spiral. Notice the diagonals? Some can be described with polynomials, which brings interesting implications about predicting prime numbers and by extension, the safety of cryptography.

We begin with a drawing area:

```
var width = 768,
  height = 768,
  svg = d3.select('#graph')
    .append('svg')
    .attr({width: width,
            height: height});
```

Then we define the algorithm that generates a list of numbers and their spiraling coordinates on a grid. We start with some helpful variables:

```
var spiral = function (n) {
  var directions = {up: [0, -1],
                    left: [-1, 0],
                    down: [0, 1],
                    right: [1, 0]};

  var x = 0,
    y = 0,
      min = [0, 0],
      max = [0, 0],
      add = [0, 0],
      direction = 0;

  var spiral = [];
});
```

We defined a `spiral` function that takes a single upper-bound argument, n. The function starts with four directions of travel and some variables for our algorithm. The combination of `min` and `max` known coordinates will tell us when to turn; x and y will be the current position, whereas `direction` will tell us which part of the spiral we're tracing.

Next we add the algorithm itself to the bottom of our function:

```
d3.range(1, n).forEach(function (i) {
    spiral.push({x: x, y: y, n: i});

    add = directions[['up', 'left', 'down', 'right'][direction]];
```

```
    x += add[0], y += add[1];

    if (x < min[0]) {
      direction = (direction+1)%4;
      min[0] = x;
    }
    if (x > max[0]) {
      direction = (direction+1)%4;
      max[0] = x;
    }
    if (y < min[1]) {
      direction = (direction+1)%4;
      min[1] = y;
    }
    if (y > max[1]) {
      direction = (direction+1)%4;
      max[1] = y;
    }
  });

  return spiral;
```

`d3.range()` generates an array of numbers between the two arguments that we iterate with `forEach`. Each iteration adds a new `{x: x, y: y, n: i}` triplet to the spiral array. The rest is just using `min` and `max` to change the direction on the spiral's corners. Yes it's repetitive, but we don't always have to be clever.

Now we get to draw stuff:

```
var dot = d3.svg.symbol().type('circle').size(3),
  center = 400,
    x = function (x, l) { return center+l*x; },
    y = function (y, l) { return center+l*y; };
```

We've defined a `dot` generator and two functions to help us turn grid coordinates from the `spiral` function into pixel positions. `l` is the length and width of a square in the grid.

We can avoid the dirty work of calculating primes by getting a list online. I found a list at `http://www.mathsisfun.com/` and placed it on GitHub next to the code examples at `https://github.com/Swizec/d3.js-book-examples/blob/master/ch3/primes-to-100k.txt`.

```
d3.text('primes-to-100k.txt', function (data) {
  var primes = data.split('\n').slice(0, 5000).map(Number),
```

```
    sequence = spiral(d3.max(primes)).filter(function (d) {
      return _.indexOf(primes, d['n'], true) > -1;
      });
  var l = 2;

  svg.selectAll('path')
    .data(sequence)
    .enter()
    .append('path')
    .attr('transform',
        function (d) { return 'translate('+x(d['x'], l)+',
'+y(d['y'], l)+')'; })
    .attr('d', dot);
});
```

We load the primes as a text file, split it into lines, use `.slice()` to get the first 5000 elements, then turn them into numbers using `.map(Number)`. We'll use l to tell the x and y functions how big the grid is.

We call `spiral` with the largest prime on our list, (`d3.max()`), to generate the spiraling sequence of numbers and then use `.filter()` to remove all non-primes from the spiral when feeding them into the drawing code.

We used `_.indexOf` of underscore.js to search for primes because it uses binary search and makes our code faster. The caveat is that we have to know our list is ordered. You can get underscore.js from `http://underscorejs.org`.

My aging machine still takes about two seconds to draw the interesting pixelated image.

Let's make it more interesting by visualizing the density of primes. We'll define a grid with larger squares, and then color them depending on how many dots they contain. Squares will be red when there are fewer primes than median, and green when there are more. The shading will tell us how far they are from the median.

First, we'll use the `nest` structure of d3.js to define a new grid:

```
var scale = 8;

var regions = d3.nest()
  .key(function (d) { return Math.floor(d['x']/scale); })
  .key(function (d) { return Math.floor(d['y']/scale); })
  .rollup(function (d) { return d.length; })
  .map(sequence);
```

We scale by a factor of 8, that is, each new square contains 64 of the old squares.

`d3.nest()` is handy for turning data into nested dictionaries according to a key. The first `.key()` function creates our columns; every x is mapped to the corresponding x of the new grid. The second `.key()` function does the same for y. We then use `.rollup()` to turn the resulting lists into a single value, a count of the dots.

The data goes in with `.map()` and we get a structure as follows:

```
{
    "0": {
        "0": 5,
        "-1": 2
    },
    "-1": {
        "0": 3,
        "-1": 4
    }
}
```

Not very self-explanatory, but that's a collection of columns containing rows. The (0, 0) square contains 5 primes, (-1, 0) contains 2, and so on.

To get the median and the number of shades, we need those counts in an array:

```
var values = d3.merge(d3.keys(regions).map(function (_x) {
        return d3.values(regions[_x]);
    }));

var median = d3.median(values),
    extent = d3.extent(values),
        shades = (extent[1]-extent[0])/2;
```

We map through the keys of our regions (x coordinates) to get a list of values for each column, and then use `d3.merge()` to flatten the resulting array of arrays.

`d3.median()` gives us the middle value of our array and `d3.extent()` gives us the lowest and highest number, which we used to calculate the number of shades we needed.

Finally, we walk the coordinates again to color the new grid:

```
d3.keys(regions).forEach(function (_x) {
    d3.keys(regions[_x]).forEach(function (_y) {

        var color,
```

```
      red = '#e23c22',
      green = '#497c36';

  if (regions[_x][_y] > median) {
    color = d3.rgb(green).brighter(regions[_x][_y]/shades);
  }else{
    color = d3.rgb(red).darker(regions[_x][_y]/shades);
  }

  svg.append('rect')
    .attr({x: x(_x, a*scale),
           y: y(_y, a*scale),
           width: a*scale,
           height: a*scale})
    .style({fill: color,
            'fill-opacity': 0.9});
  });
});
```

Our image looks like one of those Chiptunes album covers:

Loading data

One of the greatest features of d3.js is that it can asynchronously load external data without any help from third-party libraries or a programmer. We've already glanced at data loading, but it's time to take a closer look.

The reason we want to load data externally is that bootstrapping large datasets into the page with predefined variables isn't very practical. Loading hundreds of kilobytes of data takes a while and doing so asynchronously lets the rest of the page render in the meantime.

To make HTTP requests, d3.js uses XMLHttpRequests (XHR for short). This limits us to a single domain because of the browser's security model, but we can do cross-domain requests if the server sends an `Access-Control-Allow-Origin: *` header.

The core

At the core of all this loading, is the humble `d3.xhr()`, the manual way of issuing an XHR request.

It takes a URL and an optional callback. If present, the callback will immediately trigger the request and receives data as an argument once the request finishes.

If there's no callback, we get to tweak the request; everything from the headers to the request method.

To make a request you might have to write the following code:

```
var xhr = d3.xhr('<a_url>');
xhr.mimeType('application/json');
xhr.header('User-Agent', 'our example');
xhr.on('load', function (request) { … });
xhr.on('error', function (error) { … });
xhr.on('progress', function () { … });
xhr.send('GET');
```

This will send a GET request expecting a JSON response and tell the server we're an example. One way to shorten this is by defining a callback immediately, but then you can't define custom headers or listen for other request events.

Another way is convenience functions. We'll be using these throughout the book.

Convenience functions

d3.js comes with several convenience functions that use `d3.xhr()` behind the scenes, and parse the response before giving it back to us. This lets us limit our workflow to calling the appropriate function and defining a callback, which takes an `error` and a `data` argument. d3.js is nice enough to let us throw caution to the wind and use callbacks with a single `data` argument that will be undefined in case of error.

We have a choice of data formats such as TEXT, JSON, XML, HTML, CSV, and TSV. JSON and CSV/TSV are used the most: JSON for small structured data, and CSV/TSV for large data dumps where we want to conserve space.

A lot of our code will follow this kind of pattern:

```
d3.json('a_dataset.json', function (data) {
  // draw stuff
});
```

Scales

Scales are functions that map a domain to a range. Yeah, yeah, I keep saying that, but there really isn't much more to say.

The reason we use them is to avoid math. This makes our code shorter, easier to understand, and more robust as mistakes in high school mathematics are some of the hardest bugs to track down.

If you haven't just spent four years listening to mathematics at school, a function's domain are those values where it is defined (the input), and the range are those values it returns.

The following figure is borrowed from Wikipedia:

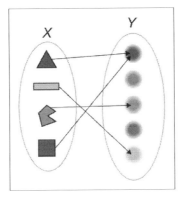

Here, **X** is the domain, **Y** is the range, and arrows are the functions.

We need a bunch of code to implement this manually:

```
var shape_color = function (shape) {
  if (shape == 'triangle') {
    return 'red';
  }else if (shape -- 'line') {
    return 'yellow';
  }else if (shape == 'pacman') {
    return 'green';
  }else if (shape == 'square') {
    return 'red';
  }
};
```

You could also do it with a dictionary, but d3.scale will always be more elegant and flexible:

```
var scale = d3.scale.ordinal()
    .domain(['triangle', 'line', 'pacman', 'square'])
    .range(['red', 'yellow', 'green', 'red']);
```

Much better!

Scales come in three types; ordinal scales have a discrete domain, quantitative scales have a continuous domain, and time scales have a time-based continuous domain.

Ordinal scales

Ordinal scales are the simplest, essentially just a dictionary where keys are the domain and values are the range.

In the preceding example, we defined an ordinal scale by explicitly setting both the input domain and the output range. If we don't define a domain, it's inferred from use, but that can give unpredictable results.

A cool thing about ordinal scales is that having a range smaller than the domain makes the scale cycle values. Furthermore, we'd get the same result if the range was just ['red', 'yellow', 'green']. But, cutting a continuous interval into chunks can make an even better range, histograms, for instance.

Let's try.

First we need a drawing area:

```
var width = 800,
  height = 600,
  svg = d3.select('#graph')
    .append('svg')
    .attr({width: width,
           height: height});
```

Then we define the three scales we need, and generate some data:

```
var data = d3.range(30),
  colors = d3.scale.category10(),
  points = d3.scale.ordinal().domain(data)
                  .rangePoints([0, height], 1.0),
  bands = d3.scale.ordinal().domain(data)
                  .rangeBands([0, width], 0.1);
```

Our data is just a list of numbers going upto 30, and the colors scale is from *Chapter 2, A Primer on DOM, SVG, and CSS*. It is a predefined ordinal scale with an undefined domain and a range of ten colors.

Then we defined two scales that split our drawing into equal parts. points uses .rangePoints() to distribute 30 equally-spaced points along the height of our drawing. We set the edge padding with a factor of 1.0, which sets the distance from the last point to the edge to half the distance between the points. End points are moved inwards from the range edge using point_distance*padding/2.

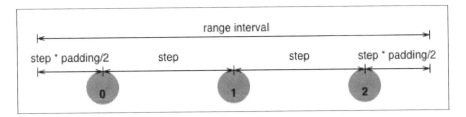

bands uses `.rangeBands()` to divide the width into `30` equal bands with a padding factor of `0.1` between bands. This time we're setting the distance between bands, using `step*padding`, and a third argument would set edge padding using `step*outerPadding`.

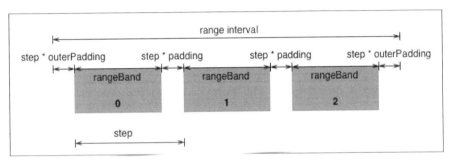

We'll use code you already know from *Chapter 2, A Primer on DOM, SVG, and CSS,* to draw two lines using these scales:

```
svg.selectAll('path')
   .data(data)
   .enter()
   .append('path')
   .attr({d: d3.svg.symbol().type('circle').size(10),
       transform: function (d) {
           return 'translate('+(width/2)+', '+points(d)+')'; }
   })
   .style('fill', function (d) { return colors(d); });

svg.selectAll('rect')
   .data(data)
   .enter()
   .append('rect')
   .attr({x: function (d) { return bands(d); },
      y: height/2,
      width: bands.rangeBand(),
      height: 10})
   .style('fill', function (d) { return colors(d); });
```

To get the positions for each dot or rectangle, we called the scales as functions and used `bands.rangeBand()` to get the rectangle width.

The picture looks as follows:

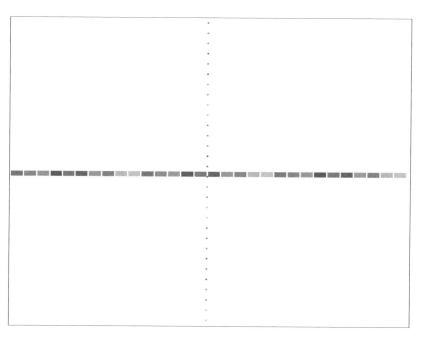

Quantitative scales

Quantitative scales come in a few different flavors, but they all share a common characteristic that the input domain is continuous. Instead of a set of discrete values, a continuous scale can be modeled with a simple function. The seven types of quantitative scales are linear, identity, power, log, quantize, quantile, and threshold. They define different transformations of the input domain. The first four have a continuous output range while the latter three map to a discrete range.

To see how they behave, we'll use all these scales to manipulate the y coordinate when drawing the `weierstrass` function; the first discovered function that is continuous everywhere but differentiable nowhere. This means that even though you can draw the function without lifting your pen, you can never define the angle you're drawing at (calculate a derivative).

We begin with a drawing area and the `weierstrass` function as found on Wikipedia is as follows:

```
var width = 800,
    height = 600,
    svg = d3.select('#graph')
      .append('svg')
      .attr({width: width,
             height: height});

var weierstrass = function (x) {
  var a = 0.5,
      b = (1+3*Math.PI/2)/a;

    return d3.sum(d3.range(100).map(function (n) {
      return Math.pow(a, n)*Math.cos(Math.pow(b, n)*Math.PI*x);
    }));
};
```

A drawing function will help us avoid code repetition:

```
var draw_one = function (line) {
  return svg.append('path')
    .datum(data)
    .attr("d", line)
    .style({'stroke-width': 2,
            fill: 'none'});
};
```

We generate some data, get the `extent` of the `weierstrass` function, and use a linear scale for x:

```
var data = d3.range(-100, 100).map(function (d) { return d/200; }),
    extent = d3.extent(data.map(weierstrass)),
    colors = d3.scale.category10(),
    x = d3.scale.linear().domain(d3.extent(data)).range([0, width]);
```

Continuous range scales

We can draw using the following code:

```
var linear = d3.scale.linear().domain(extent).range([height/4, 0]),
    line1 = d3.svg.line()
      .x(x)
      .y(function(d) { return linear(weierstrass(d)); });
```

```
draw_one(line1)
    .attr('transform', 'translate(0, '+(height/16)+')')
    .style('stroke', colors(0));
```

We defined a linear scale with the domain encompassing all the values returned by the `weierstrass` function, and a range from zero to the drawing width. The scale will use linear interpolation to translate between the input and the output, and will even predict values that fall outside its domain. If we don't want that happening, we can use `.clamp()`. Using more than two numbers in the domain and range, we can create a polylinear scale where each section behaves like a separate linear scale.

The linear scale creates the following screenshot:

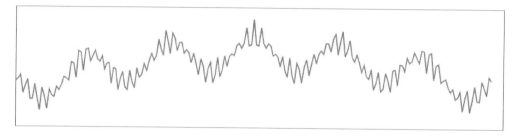

Let's add the other continuous scales in one fell swoop:

```
var identity = d3.scale.identity().domain(extent),
    line2 = line1.y(function (d) { return identity(weierstrass(d)); });

draw_one(line2)
    .attr('transform', 'translate(0, '+(height/12)+')')
    .style('stroke', colors(1));

var power = d3.scale.pow().exponent(0.2).domain(extent).
range([height/2, 0]),
    line3 = line1.y(function (d) { return power(weierstrass(d)); });

draw_one(line3)
    .attr('transform', 'translate(0, '+(height/8)+')')
    .style('stroke', colors(2));

var log = d3.scale.log().domain(
    d3.extent(data.filter(function (d) { return d > 0 ? d : 0; }))).
range([0, width]),
    line4 = line1.x(function (d) { return d > 0 ? log(d) : 0; })
        .y(function (d) { return linear(weierstrass(d)); });
```

```
draw_one(line4)
    .attr('transform', 'translate(0, '+(height/4)+')')
    .style('stroke', colors(3));
```

We keep re-using the same `line` definition, changing the scale used for `y`, except for the `power` scale, because changing `x` makes a better example.

We also took into account that `log` is only defined on positive numbers, but you usually wouldn't use it for periodic functions anyway. It's much better at showing large and small numbers on the same graph.

Now our picture looks as follows:

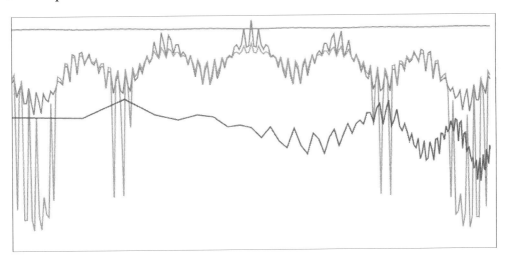

The `identity` scale is orange and wiggles around by barely a pixel because the data we feed into the function only goes from -0.5 to 0.5, the `power` scale is green, and the `logarithmic` scale is red.

Discrete range scales

The interesting scales for our comparison are `quantize` and `threshold`. The `quantize` scale cuts the input domain into equal parts and maps them to values in the output range, while `threshold` scales let us map arbitrary domain sections to discrete values:

```
var quantize = d3.scale.quantize().domain(extent)
                        .range(d3.range(-1, 2, 0.5).map(function (d) {
    return d*100; })),
```

```
    line5 = line1.x(x).y(function (d) { return quantize(weierstrass(d));
  }),
    offset = 100

draw_one(line5)
  .attr('transform', 'translate(0, '+(height/2+offset)+')')
  .style('stroke', colors(4));

var threshold = d3.scale.threshold().domain([-1, 0, 1]).range([-50, 0,
50, 100]),
  line6 = line1.x(x).y(function (d) { return
threshold(weierstrass(d)); });

draw_one(line6)
  .attr('transform', 'translate(0, '+(height/2+offset*2)+')')
  .style('stroke', colors(5));
```

The `quantize` scale will divide the `weierstrass` function into discrete values between 1 and 2 with a step of 0.5 (-1, -0.5, 0, and so on), and threshold will map values smaller than -1 to -50, -1 to 0, and so on.

The result looks as follows:

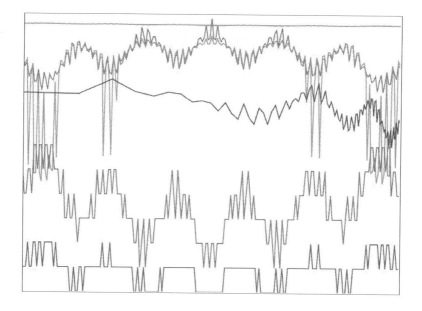

Time

You don't understand time. You might think you do, but you don't.

Keep this in mind next time you want to add 3,600 seconds to a timestamp to advance it by an hour, or basically `now+24*3600` is tomorrow.

Time is a complicated beast. An hour can last 3600 seconds or 3599 seconds, if there's a leap second. Tomorrow can be 23 to 25 hours away, months range from 28 to 31 days, and a year can be 365 or 366 days. Some decades have fewer days than others.

Considering many datasets are closely tied to time, this can become a big problem. Just how do you handle time?

Luckily, d3.js comes with a bunch of time-handling features.

Formatting

You can create a new formatter by giving `d3.time.format()` a format string. You can then use it for parsing strings into `Date` objects and vice-versa.

The whole language is explained in the documentation of d3.js, but let's look at a few examples:

```
> format = d3.time.format('%Y-%m-%d')
> format.parse('2012-02-19')
Sun Feb 19 2012 00:00:00 GMT+0100 (CET)
```

We defined a new formatter with `d3.time.format()` (year-month-day), then parsed a date as they often appear in datasets. This gave us a proper `date` object with default values for hours, minutes, and seconds.

The same formatter works the other way:

```
> format(new Date())
"2013-02-19"
```

You can find the full ISO standard time formatter at `d3.time.format.iso`. That often comes in handy.

Time arithmetic

We also get a full suite of time arithmetic functions that work with JavaScript's `Date` objects and follow a few simple rules:

1. `d3.time.interval`, where `interval` can be a `second`, `minute`, `hour`, and so on. It returns a new time interval. For instance, `d3.time.hour` will be an hour long.

2. `d3.time.interval(Date)`, is an alias for `interval.floor()`, which rounds `Date` down so that more specific units than the `interval` are set to zero.

3. `interval.offset(Date, step)`, will move the date by a specified number of steps to the correct unit.

4. `interval.range(Date_start, Date_stop)`, will return every `interval` between the two specified dates.

5. `d3.time.intervals`, where an `interval` is seconds, minutes, hours, and so on. They are helpful aliases for `interval.range`.

For instance, if you want to find the time an hour from now, you'd do this:

```
> d3.time.hour.offset(new Date(), 1)
Tue Feb 19 2013 06:09:17 GMT+0100 (CET)
```

And find out it's getting really late and you should stop writing books about JavaScript, and go to bed.

Geography

Other useful data types are geospatial coordinates, often used for weather or population data; anything where you want to draw a map.

d3.js gives us three tools for geographic data: paths produce the final pixels, projections turn sphere coordinates into Cartesian coordinates, and streams speed things up.

The main data format we'll use is TopoJSON, a more compact extension of GeoJSON, created by Mike Bostock. In a way, TopoJSON is to GeoJSON what DivX is to video. While GeoJSON uses the JSON format to encode geographical data with points, lines, and polygons, TopoJSON instead encodes basic features with arcs and re-uses them to build more and more complex features. As a result, files can be as much as 80 percent smaller than when we use GeoJSON.

Getting geodata

Now, unlike many other datasets, geodata can't be found just lying around the Internet. Especially not in a fringe format such as TopoJSON. We'll find some data in Shapefile or GeoJSON formats, and then use the `topojson` command-line utility to transform them into TopoJSON. Finding detailed data can be difficult, but is not impossible, look for your country's census bureau. For instance, the US Census Bureau has many useful datasets available at `http://www.census.gov/geo/www/cob/index.html`.

Natural Earth is another magnificent resource for geodata at different levels of detail. The biggest advantage is that different layers (oceans, countries, roads, and so on) are carefully made to fit together without discrepancies and are frequently updated. You can find the datasets at `http://www.naturalearthdata.com/`.

Let's prepare some data for the next example. Go to `http://www.naturalearthdata.com/` and download the `ocean`, `land`, `rivers and lake centerlines`, and `land boundary lines` datasets at 50m detail level, and the `urban areas` dataset at 10m. You'll find them in the **Downloads** tab. The files are also in the examples on GitHub available at `https://github.com/Swizec/d3.js-book-examples/tree/master/ch3/data`.

Unzip the five files. We'll combine them into three TopoJSON files to save the request time, three big files are quicker than five small files, and we prefer TopoJSON because of the smaller file size.

We'll merge categorically so that we can reuse the files later; one for water data, another for land data, and a third for cultural data.

You'll need to install `topojson`, which needs node.js. Follow the installation instructions for your computer on `nodejs.org`, then open a terminal, and run this command:

```
> npm install -global topojson
```

npm is node's built-in package manager. It downloads and installs the `topojson` library globally. You might have to run this as a super user.

Next, we transform the files with three simple commands:

```
> topojson -o water.json ne_50m_rivers_lake_centerlines.shp ne_50m_ocean.shp
> topojson -o land.json ne_50m_land.shp
> topojson -o cultural.json ne_50m_admin_0_boundary_lines.shp ne_10m_urban_areas.shp
```

The `topojson` library transforms shape files into TopoJSON files and merges the files we wanted. We specified where to put the results with `-o`; the other arguments were source files.

We've generated three files: `water.json`, `land.json`, and `cultural.json`. Feel free to look at them, but they aren't very human-friendly.

Drawing geographically

`d3.geo.path()` is going to be the work horse of our geographic drawings. It's similar to the SVG path generators we learned about earlier, except it draws geographic data and is smart enough to decide whether to draw a line or an area.

To flatten spherical objects such as planets into a 2D image, `d3.geo.path()` uses projections. Different kinds of projections are designed to showcase different things about the data, but the end result is you can completely change what the map looks like, just by changing the projection or moving its focal point.

With the right projection you can even make the data of Europe look like the U.S. Rather unfortunately then, the default projection is `albersUsa` designed specifically to draw the standard map of U.S.

Let's draw a map of the world, centered and zoomed into Europe because that's where I'm from. We'll make it navigable in *Chapter 4, Making Things Move*.

We first need to add some things to our standard HTML file.

Add an empty `style` definition above the main div; we'll use it later to make our map look better:

```
<style></style>
```

We also need two more JavaScript files right after d3.js:

```
<script src="http://d3js.org/topojson.v0.min.js"></script>
<script src="http://d3js.org/queue.v1.min.js"></script>
```

These load the TopoJSON parser and a queue utility to help us load more than one dataset.

We continue in our JavaScript file with a drawing area:

```
var width = 1800,
  height = 1200,
  svg = d3.select('#graph')
    .append('svg')
    .attr({width: width,
           height: height});
```

Next, we define a geographic `projection`:

```
var projection = d3.geo.equirectangular()
    .center([8, 56])
    .scale(800);
```

The `equirectangular` projection is one of the twelve projections that come with d3.js, and is perhaps the most common projection we're used to seeing ever since high school.

The problem with `equirectangular` is that it doesn't preserve areas or represent the earth's surface all that well. A full discussion of projecting a sphere onto a two dimensional surface would take too much time, so I suggest looking at the Wikipedia page of d3.js and the visual comparison of all the projections implemented in the projection plugin. It is available at `https://github.com/mbostock/d3/wiki/Geo-Projections`.

The next two lines define where our map is centered and how zoomed in it is. By fiddling I got all three values latitude of `8`, longitude of `56`, and a scaling factor of `800`. Play around to get a different look.

Now we load our data:

```
queue()
  .defer(d3.json, 'data/water.json')
  .defer(d3.json, 'data/land.json')
  .defer(d3.json, 'data/cultural.json')
  .await(draw);
```

We're using Mike Bostock's `queue` library to run the three loading operations in sequence. Each will use `d3.json` to load and parse the data, and when they're all done, `queue` will call `draw` with the results.

We need one more thing before we start drawing; a function that adds a feature to the map, which will help us reduce code repetition:

```
function add_to_map(collection, key) {
  return svg.append('g')
    .selectAll('path')
    .data(topojson.object(collection,
                 collection.objects[key]).geometries)
      .enter()
    .append('path')
    .attr('d', d3.geo.path().projection(projection));
}
```

This function takes a collection of objects and a key to choose which object to display. `topojson.object()` translates a TopoJSON topology into a GeoJSON one for `d3.geo.path()`.

Whether it's more efficient to transform to GeoJSON than transferring data in the target representation depends on your use case. Transforming data takes some computational time, but transferring megabytes instead of kilobytes can make a big difference in responsiveness.

Finally, we create a new `d3.geo.path()`, and tell it to use our projection. Other than generating the SVG path string, `d3.geo.path()` can also calculate different properties of our feature, such as the area (`.area()`) and the bounding box (`.bounds()`).

Now we can start drawing:

```
function draw (err, water, land, cultural) {
  add_to_map(water, 'ne_50m_ocean')
    .classed('ocean', true);
};
```

Our `draw` function takes the error returned from loading data, and the three datasets then lets `add_to_map` do the heavy lifting.

Add some styling to the HTML:

```
.ocean {
  fill: #759dd1;
}
```

Refreshing the page will reveal some oceans.

We add four more `add_to_map` calls to the `draw` function to fill in the other features:

```
add_to_map(land, 'ne_50m_land')
  .classed('land', true);

add_to_map(water, 'ne_50m_rivers_lake_centerlines')
  .classed('river', true);

add_to_map(cultural, 'ne_50m_admin_0_boundary_lines_land')
  .classed('boundary', true);

add_to_map(cultural, 'ne_10m_urban_areas')
  .classed('urban', true);
```

Add some style definitions as follows:

```
.river {
  fill: none;
  stroke: #759dd1;
  stroke-width: 1;
}
```

```
.land {
  fill: #ede9c9;
  stroke: #79bcd3;
  stroke-width: 2;
}

.boundary {
  stroke: #7b5228;
  stroke-width: 1;
  fill: none;
}

.urban {
  fill: #e1c0a3;
}
```

We now have a slowly rendering world map zoomed into Europe, displaying the world's urban areas as blots:

There are many reasons why it's so slow. We transform between TopoJSON and GeoJSON on every call to add_to_map. Even when using the same dataset, we're using data that's too detailed for such a zoomed out map, and we render the whole world to look at a tiny part. We traded flexibility for rendering speed.

Using geography as a base

Geography isn't just about drawing maps. A map is usually a base we build to show some data.

Let's turn this into a map of the world's airports. I wanted to make a map of the routes between airports at first, but it looked too crowded.

The first step is fetching the `airports.dat` and `routes.dat` datasets from `http://openflights.org/data.html`. You can also find it in the examples on GitHub at `https://github.com/Swizec/d3.js-book-examples/blob/master/ch3/data/airports.dat`.

Add a call to `add_airlines()` at the bottom of `draw`. We'll use it to load more data and draw the airports:

```
function add_airlines() {
  queue()
    .defer(d3.text, 'data/airports.dat')
    .defer(d3.text, 'data/routes.dat')
    .await(draw_airlines);
};
```

The function loads the two datasets, and then calls `draw_airlines` to draw them. We use `d3.text` instead of `d3.csv` because the files don't have a header line so we have to parse them manually.

In `draw_airlines`, we first wrangle the data into JavaScript objects, airports into a dictionary by `id`, and routes into a mapping of source to the target airport:

```
function draw_airlines(err, _airports, _routes) {
  var airports = {},
    routes = {};

  d3.csv.parseRows(_airports).forEach(function (airport) {
    var id = airport[0];

    airports[id] = {
      lat: airport[6],
      lon: airport[7]
    };
  });

  d3.csv.parseRows(_routes).forEach(function (route) {
    var from_airport = route[3];
```

```
        if (!routes[from_airport]) {
          routes[from_airport] = [];
        }

        routes[from_airport].push({
          to: route[5],
          from: from_airport,
          stops: route[7]
        });
      });
    }
```

We used d3.csv.parseRows to parse CSV files into arrays and manually turned them into dictionaries. The array indices aren't very legible unfortunately, but they make sense when you look at the raw data:

```
1,"Goroka","Goroka","Papua New Guinea","GKA","AYGA",-
6.081689,145.391881,5282,10,"U"
2,"Madang","Madang","Papua New Guinea","MAG","AYMD",-
5.207083,145.7887,20,10,"U"
```

The radius of each airport circle will show how many routes are leaving from it. So, we need a scale:

```
var route_N = d3.values(routes).map(function (routes) {
    return routes.length;
  }),
    r = d3.scale.linear().domain(d3.extent(route_N)).range([2, 15]);
```

We took an array of route counts and turned it into a linear scale.

Now we can draw the airports:

```
svg.append('g')
    .selectAll('circle')
    .data(d3.keys(airports))
    .enter()
    .append('circle')
    .attr("transform", function (id) {
      var airport = airports[id];
      return "translate("+projection([airport.lon, airport.lat])+")";
    })
    .attr('r', function (id) { return routes[id] ? r(routes[id].
length) : 1; })
    .classed('airport', true);
```

The tricky part is that we used the same `projection` we gave to `d3.geo.path()` to turn airport positions into circle coordinates. We avoided the `cx` and `cy` attributes so that we can take advantage of `projection` working on two coordinates at once. By now, everything else should be familiar from *Chapter 2, A Primer on DOM, SVG, and CSS*.

Airports without routes will be very small dots.

Later we add some more CSS to our HTML:

```
.airport {
  fill: #9e56c7;
  opacity: 0.6;
  stroke: #69349d;
}
```

The following screenshot displays the result:

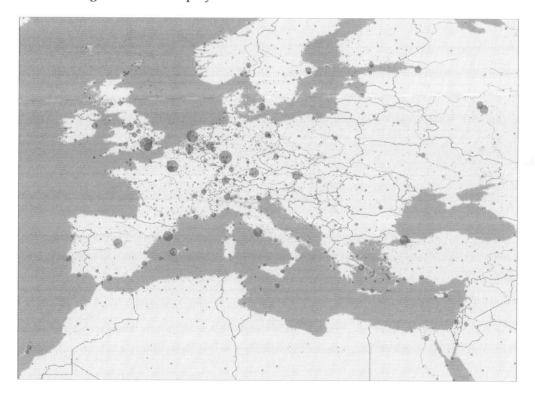

Summary

You've made it through the chapter on data!

We really got to the core of what d3.js is about, that is, data wrangling. The part about functional programming hopefully inspired you to take up functional-style programming, if you were still on the fence. Learning about data wrangling we saw some interesting properties of prime numbers, learned all about loading external data, and effectively used scales to avoid calculation.

Finally, we made a cool map to learn how simple geographic data can be once you get a hand on a good source and transform it into a better format.

4
Making Things Move

A pretty picture is just the beginning! The hallmark of taking full advantage of the medium is making visualizations that adapt to new situations. Visualizations that let the user explore our data.

In this chapter, we'll animate our pictures with the powerful transitions module of d3.js, and will look at some strategies for interacting with the user.

Animating with transitions

So far attributes have been applied instantly, which is great for rendering an image, but what if we want to highlight something with a simple animation? Perhaps we just want a smoother transition from nothing to "Hey, graph!" while loading external data?

That's where transitions come in. Transitions use the familiar principle of changing a selection's attributes, except that changes are applied over time.

To slowly turn a rectangle red, we'd use the following line of code:

```
d3.select('rect').transition().style('fill', 'red');
```

We start a new transition with `.transition()` and then define the final state of each animated attribute. By default, every transition takes 250 milliseconds; you can change the timing with `.duration()`. New transitions are executed on all properties simultaneously unless you set a delay using `.delay()`.

Delays are handy when we want to make transitions happen in sequence. Without a delay, they are all executed at the same time, depending on an internal timer.

For single objects, nested transitions are much simpler than carefully calibrated delays.

Take our rectangle example and write something like this in your Chrome console. If you haven't already, you'll need to actually add a rectangle to the page for this to work. Such is life.

```
d3.select('rect')
    .transition().style('fill', 'red').attr('x', 200)
    .transition().attr('y', 200)
```

Running this code, you'll see the rectangle become red as it moves right by a hundred pixels, then moves downwards by the same distance.

Capturing animations in screenshots is tough, but say this is your initial state:

The final state would look like this:

We do realize these are just two squares on a white background, but believe me, the red square is a hundred pixels below and to the right of the black square.

If you want to do something before a transition begins, or want to listen for it to end, you can use `.each()` with the appropriate event type like this:

```
rect.transition()
    .style('fill', 'red')
    .each('start', function () { console.log("stahp, you're making me
blush"); })
    .each('end', function () { console.log("crap, I'm all red now");
})
```

This is handy for making instant changes before or after a transition. Just keep in mind that transitions run independently and you cannot rely on transitions outside the current callback being in this state or that.

Interpolators

To calculate values between the initial and final states of a transition, d3.js uses interpolators—functions mapping the `[0,1]` domain to the target range (color, number, or string). Under the hood, scales are based on these same interpolators.

D3's built-in interpolators can interpolate between almost any two arbitrary values, most often between numbers or colors, but also between strings. This sounds odd at first, but it's actually pretty useful.

To let d3.js pick the right interpolator for the job, we just write `d3.interpolate(a, b)` and the `interpolation` function is chosen depending on the type of `b`.

If `b` is a number, `a` will be coerced into a number and `.interpolateNumber()` will be used. You should avoid interpolating to or from a zero value because values will eventually be transformed into a string for the actual attribute and very small numbers might turn into scientific notation. CSS and HTML don't quite understand `1e-7` (the digit 1 with seven zeroes in front), so the smallest number you can safely use is `1e-6`.

If `b` is a string, d3.js checks whether it's a CSS color, in which case it is transformed to a proper color, just like the ones in *Chapter 2, A Primer on DOM, SVG, and CSS*. `a` is transformed into a color as well, and then d3.js uses `.interpolateRgb()` or a more appropriate interpolator for your color space.

Something even more amazing happens when the string is not a color. d3.js can handle that too! When it encounters a string, d3.js will parse it for numbers, then use `.interpolateNumber()` on each numerical piece of the string. This is useful for interpolating mixed style definitions.

For instance, to transition a font definition, you might do something like this:

```
d3.select('svg')
    .append('text')
    .attr({x: 100, y: 100})
    .text("I'm growing!")
    .transition()
    .styleTween('font', function () {
        return d3.interpolate('12px Helvetica', '36px Comic Sans MS');
```

We used `.styleTween()` to manually define a transition. It is most useful when we want to define the starting value of a transition without relying on the current state. The first argument defines which style attribute to transition and the second is the interpolator.

You can use `.tween()` to do this for attributes other than style.

Every numerical part of the string was interpolated between the starting and ending values, and the string parts changed to their final state immediately. An interesting application of this is interpolating path definitions—you can make shapes change in time. How cool is that?

Keep in mind that only strings with the same number and location of control points (numbers in the string) can be interpolated. You can't use interpolators for everything. Creating a custom interpolator is as simple as defining a function that takes a single `t` parameter and returns the start value for $t = 0$ and end value for $t = 1$ and blends values for anything in between.

For example, the following code shows the `interpolateNumber` function of d3.js:

```
function interpolateNumber(a, b) {
    return function(t) {
        return a + t * (b - a);
    };
}
```

It's as simple as that!

You can even interpolate whole arrays and objects, which work like compound interpolators of multiple values. We'll use those soon.

Easing

Easing tweaks the behavior of interpolators by controlling the t argument. We use this to make our animations feel more natural, to add some bounce elasticity, and so on. Mostly we use easing to avoid the artificial feel of linear animation.

Let's make a quick comparison of the easing functions provided by d3.js and see what they do.

Don't forget the drawing area! I once spent an hour debugging a graph before realizing there was no svg element.

```
var width = 1024,
  height = 768,
  svg = d3.select('#graph')
    .append('svg')
    .attr({width: width,
           height: height});
```

Next, we need an array of easing functions and a scale for placing them along the vertical axis.

```
var eases = ['linear', 'poly(4)', 'quad', 'cubic', 'sin', 'exp',
'circle', 'elastic(10, -5)', 'back(0.5)', 'bounce', 'cubic-in',
'cubic-out', 'cubic-in-out', 'cubic-out-in'],
    y = d3.scale.ordinal().domain(eases).rangeBands([50, 500]);
```

You'll notice that poly, elastic, and back take arguments; since these are just strings, we'll have to manually change them into real arguments later. The poly easing function is just a polynomial, so poly(2) is equal to quad and poly(3) is equal to cubic.

The elastic easing function simulates an elastic and the two arguments control tension. I suggest playing with the values to get the effect you want.

The back easing function is supposed to simulate backing into a parking space. The argument controls how much overshoot there's going to be.

The nonsense at the end (cubic-in, cubic-out, and so on) is a list of the easing functions we create ourselves by combining the following modifiers:

* -in: It does nothing
* -out: It reverses the easing direction

- -in-out: It copies and mirrors the easing function from [0, 0.5] and [0.5, 1]

- -out-in: It copies and mirrors the easing function from [1, 0.5] and [0.5, 0]

You can add these to any easing function, so play around. Time to render a circle flying towards the right for every function in the list:

```
eases.forEach(function (ease) {
    var transition = svg.append('circle')
        .attr({cx: 130,
            cy: y(ease),
            r: y.rangeBand()/2-5})
        .transition()
        .delay(400)
        .duration(1500)
        .attr({cx: 400});
});
```

We loop over the list with an iterator that creates a new circle and uses the y() scale for vertical placement and y.rangeBand() for circle size. This way, we can add or remove examples easily. Transitions will start with a delay of just under half a second to give us a chance to see what's going on. A duration of 1500 milliseconds and a final position of 400 should give enough time and space to see the easing.

We define the easing at the end of this function, before the }); bit:

```
if (ease.indexOf('(') > -1) {
    var args = ease.match(/[0-9]+/g),
        type = ease.match(/^[a-z]+/);

    transition.ease(type, args[0], args[1]);
}else{
    transition.ease(ease);
}
```

This code checks for parentheses in the ease string, parses out the easing function and its arguments, and feeds them to transition.ease(). Without parentheses, ease is just the easing type.

Let's add some text so we can tell the examples apart:

```
svg.append('text')
    .text(ease)
    .attr({x: 10,
        y: y(ease)+5});
```

The visualization is a cacophony of dots:

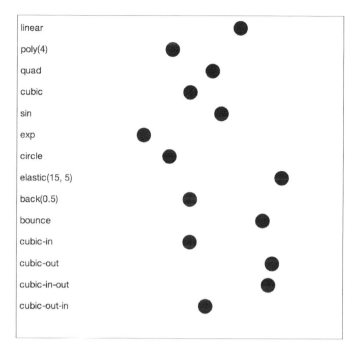

The screenshot doesn't quite showcase the animation, so you should really try this one in the browser. Or you can take a look at the easing curves at http://easings.net/.

Timers

To schedule transitions, d3.js uses timers. Even an immediate transition will start after a delay of 17 ms.

Far from keeping timers all to itself, d3.js lets us use timers so that we can take animation beyond the two-keyframe model of transition. For those of us who aren't animators, keyframes define the start or end of a smooth transition.

To create a timer, we use d3.timer(). It takes a function, a delay, and a starting mark. After the set delay (in milliseconds) from the mark, the function will be executed repeatedly until it returns true. The mark should be a date converted into milliseconds since Unix epoch (Date.getTime() will do), or you can let d3.js use Date.now() by default.

Let's animate the drawing of a parametric function to work just like the Spirograph toy you might have had as a kid.

We'll create a timer, let it run for a few seconds, and use the millisecond mark as the parameter for a parametric function.

First we need a drawing area:

```
var width = 600,
    height = 600,
    svg = d3.select('#graph')
        .append('svg')
        .attr({width: width,
               height: height});
```

I found a good function in Wikipedia's article on parametric equations at http://en.wikipedia.org/wiki/Parametric_equations.

```
var position = function (t) {
    var a = 80, b = 1, c = 1, d = 80;

    return {x: Math.cos(a*t) - Math.pow(Math.cos(b*t), 3),
            y: Math.sin(c*t) - Math.pow(Math.sin(d*t), 3)};
};
```

This function will return a mathematical position based on the parameter going from zero up. You can tweak the Spirograph by changing the a, b, c, and d variables—examples in the same Wikipedia article.

This function returns positions between -2 and 2, so we need some scales to make it visible on the screen:

```
var t_scale = d3.scale.linear().domain([500, 25000]).range([0, 2*Math.
PI]),
    x = d3.scale.linear().domain([-2, 2]).range([100, width-100]),
    y = d3.scale.linear().domain([-2, 2]).range([height-100, 100]);
```

t_scale will translate time into parameters for the function; x and y will calculate the final position on the image.

Now we need to define brush to fly around and pretend it's drawing and a variable to hold the previous position so that we can draw straight lines.

```
var brush = svg.append('circle')
        .attr({r: 4}),
    previous = position(0);
```

Next, we need to define an animation `step` function that moves the brush and draws a line between the previous and current points:

```
var step = function (time) {
  if (time > t_scale.domain()[1]) {
    return true;
  }

  var t = t_scale(time),
    pos = position(t);

  brush.attr({cx: x(pos.x),
              cy: y(pos.y)});
  svg.append('line')
    .attr({x1: x(previous.x),
           y1: y(previous.y),
           x2: x(pos.x),
           y2: y(pos.y),
           stroke: 'steelblue',
           'stroke-width': 1.3});

  previous = pos;
};
```

The first condition stops the timer when the current value of the `time` parameter is beyond the domain of `t_scale`. Then, we use `t_scale()` to translate the time into our parameter and get a new position for the brush.

Then, we move the brush—there is no transition because *we* are performing the transition—and draw a new steelblue line between the previous and current position (`pos`).

We conclude by setting a new value for the previous position.

All that's left now is creating a timer:

```
var timer = d3.timer(step, 500);
```

That's it. Half a second after a page refresh, the code will begin drawing a beautiful shape and finish 25 seconds later.

Starting out, it looks like this:

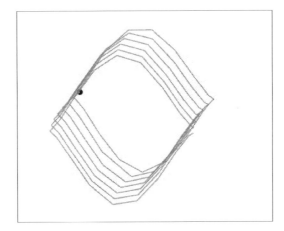

Getting the whole picture takes a while, so this probably isn't the best way to draw Spirographs. Since we're using time as a parameter, a smoother curve (more points) takes more time.

Another problem is that lagging computers or slower machines will affect the final outcome of the animation.

A reader wrote a version without these problems and put the code on Github at `https://github.com/johnaho/d3.js-book-examples/blob/master/ch4/timers.js`.

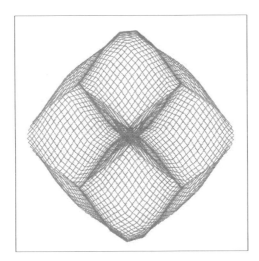

But both versions of the code will eventually come up with a beautiful flower. When I wrote this code, I spent an hour just marveling at the drawing process and tweaking the parameters to see what happens.

Interacting with the user

Great visualizations don't just stop at pretty pictures and animations! They give users the power to play with data and figure things out on their own. That's what we'll look into next.

You don't know it yet, but you already know how to let users interact with visualizations.

Basic interaction

Much like with other UI libraries, the principle for interaction is simple—attach an event listener to an element and do something when it's triggered. We add and remove listeners to and from selections with the `.on()` method, an event type (for instance, `click`), and a listener function that is executed when the event is triggered.

We can set a capture flag, which ensures our listener is called first and all other listeners wait for our listener to finish. Events bubbling up from children elements will not trigger our listener.

You can rely on the fact there will only ever be a single listener for a particular event on an element because old listeners for the same event are removed when new ones are added. This is very useful for avoiding unpredictable behavior.

Just like other functions acting on element selections, event listeners get the current datum and index and set the `this` context to the DOM element. The global `d3.event` will let you access the actual event object.

Let's play around with these principles and a simple visualization using mouse clicks and finger touches. Yes, d3.js has some support for touch devices, but it doesn't always work perfectly.

As always, begin with a drawing area:

```
var width = 1024,
  height = 768,
  svg = d3.select('#graph')
    .append('svg')
    .attr({width: width,
           height: height});
```

Next, we create a function that will emulate ripples in a pond using three circles; you might need some imagination:

```
var radiate = function (pos) {
  d3.range(3).forEach(function (d) {
    svg.append('circle')
      .attr({cx: pos[0],
             cy: pos[1],
             r: 0})
      .style('opacity', '1')
      .transition()
      .duration(1000)
      .delay(d*50)
       .attr('r', 50)
       .style('opacity', '0.00001')
       .remove();
  });
};
```

The `radiate` function creates three circles centered around a position, defined by a two-element array — [x, y]. A transition will grow the circles, reduce their opacity, and in the end, remove them. We used `.delay` to ensure the circles don't overlap, which creates the rippling illusion.

Now for the fun part:

```
svg.on('click', function () {
  radiate(d3.mouse(this));
});

svg.on('touchstart', function () {
  d3.touches(this).map(radiate);
});
```

We used `.on()` once for each type of event we want to make ripples for — the familiar `click` event first and then the possibly less familiar `touchstart`. The `touchstart` event is triggered when a finger touches the screen; think of it as the `mousedown` event of touch. Other useful touch events are `touchmove`, `touchend`, `touchcancel`, and `tap`. Mozilla's documentation explains touch events in more detail at `https://developer.mozilla.org/en-US/docs/Web/Guide/API/DOM/Events/Touch_events`.

The `click` listener uses `d3.mouse()` to get the cursor's position relative to the container element, and the `touchstart` listener maps through a list of all touches. In theory, this will draw several ripples if you smoosh your whole hand on the screen, but I was unable to get this working on any of my devices.

Make the ripples pretty with some styling:

```
<style>
circle {
    fill: none;
    stroke: red;
    stroke-width: 2;
}
</style>
```

Clicking around makes ripples!

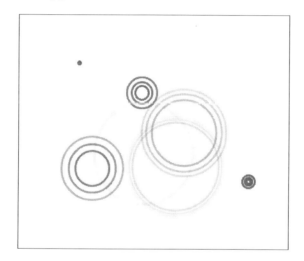

Behaviors

Sometimes, you want more than to just let the user click around like a madman; you want drag-and-drop and zoom-in and zoom-out stuff!

You can make all this with just click events, but I heartily recommend d3's behaviors module. It makes complex behaviors as simple as calling the right function on some elements.

Currently, d3.js supports only `drag` and `zoom`, but I am hopeful that more are on the way. The main benefit of behaviors is that they automatically create relevant event listeners and let you work at a higher level of abstraction.

Drag

I can't think of a better dragging demonstration than animating with the parallax illusion. The illusion works by having several keyframes rendered in vertical slices and dragging a screen over them to create an animated thingamabob.

Drawing the lines by hand would be tedious, so we're using an image *Marco Kuiper* created in Photoshop. I asked on Twitter and he said we can use the image, if we check out his other work at marcofolio.net.

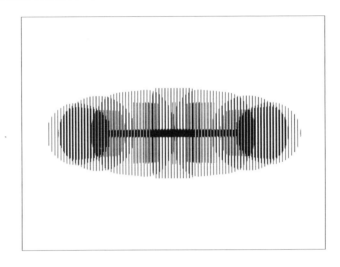

You can also get the image in the examples repository at https://raw.github.com/Swizec/d3.js-book-examples/master/ch4/parallax_base.png.

We need somewhere to put the parallax:

```
var width = 1200,
  height = 450,
  svg = d3.select('#graph')
    .append('svg')
    .attr({width: width,
          height: height});
```

We'll use SVG's native support for embedding bitmaps to insert parallax_base.png into the page:

```
svg.append('image')
  .attr({'xlink:href': 'parallax_base.png',
        width: width,
        height: height});
```

The `image` element's magic stems from its `xlink:href` attribute. It understands links and even lets us embed images to create self-contained SVGs. To use that, you would prepend an image MIME type to a base64 encoded representation of the image.

For instance, the following line is the smallest embedded version of a spacer GIF. Don't worry if you don't know what a spacer GIF is; they were useful up to about 2005.

```
data:image/gif;base64,R0lGODlhAQABAID/
AMDAwAAAACH5BAEAAAAALAAAAABAAEAAAICRAEAOw==
```

Anyway, now that we have the animation base, we need a screen that can be dragged. It's going to be a bunch of carefully calibrated vertical lines:

```
var screen_width = 900,
  lines = d3.range(screen_width/6),
  x = d3.scale.ordinal().domain(lines).rangeBands([0, screen_width]);
```

We'll base the screen off an array of numbers (`lines`). Since line thickness and density are very important, we divide `screen_width` by 6—five pixels for a line and one for spacing. Make sure the value of `screen_width` is a multiple of 6; otherwise anti-aliasing ruins the effect.

The x scale will help us place the lines evenly.

```
svg.append('g')
  .selectAll('line')
  .data(lines)
  .enter()
  .append('line')
  .style('shape-rendering', 'crispEdges')
  .attr({stroke: 'black',
        'stroke-width': x.rangeBand()-1,
        x1: function (d) { return x(d); },
        y1: 0,
        x2: function (d) { return x(d); },
        y2: height});
```

There's nothing particularly interesting here, just stuff you already know. The code goes through the array and draws a new vertical line for each entry. We made absolutely certain there won't be any anti-aliasing by setting `shape-rendering` to `crispEdges`.

Time to define and activate a dragging behavior for our group of lines:

```
var drag = d3.behavior.drag()
    .origin(Object)
    .on('drag', function () {
        d3.select(this)
            .attr('transform', 'translate('+d3.event.x+', 0)')
            .datum({x: d3.event.x, y: 0});
    });
```

We created the behavior with `d3.behavior.drag()`, defined a `.origin()` accessor, and specified what happens on drag. The behavior automatically translates touch and mouse events to the higher-level drag event. How cool is that!

We need to give the behavior an origin so it knows how to calculate positions relatively; otherwise, the current position is always set to the mouse cursor and objects jump around. It's terrible. `Object` is the identity function for elements and assumes a datum with *x* and *y* coordinates.

The heavy lifting happens inside the `drag` listener. We get the screen's new position from `d3.event.x`, move the screen there, and update the attached `.datum()` method.

All that's left to do is to call `drag` and make sure to set the attached datum to the current position:

```
svg.select('g')
    .datum({x: 0, y: 0})
    .call(drag);
```

The item looks solid now! Try dragging the screen at different speeds.

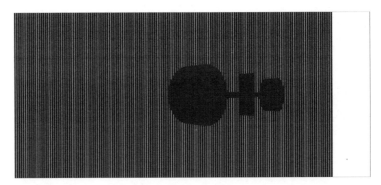

The parallax effect doesn't work very well on a retina display because the base image gets resized and our screen loses calibration.

Zoom

Despite the name, the zoom behavior lets you do more than just zoom—you can also pan! Like the drag behavior, zoom automatically handles both mouse and touch events and then triggers the higher-level zoom event. Yes, this means pinch-to-zoom works! That's pretty awesome if you ask me.

Remember that map from *Chapter 3, Making Data Useful*? The one with airports on a world map? That one.

Let's commit a crime against computational efficiency and make it zoom and pan.

I am warning you this will be very rudimentary and painfully slow. This is not how you'd make a real explorable map, just an example to let us play with zooming. In real life you should use tiling, progressive detailing, and other tricks.

To make this a bit more bearable, you should disable water and urban areas. Comment out add_to_map calls for rivers, lakes, and oceans roughly on lines 30, 36, and 42 in the JavaScript code.

Your map becomes much simpler:

The biggest effect comes from removing large areas, so if you remove land as well, the map will be surprisingly performant but quite useless.

Jump to the end of `draw_airlines` and add a call to `zoomable`; we'll define this next:

```
zoomable(airports, R, routes);
```

`zoomable` needs `airports`, `R_scale`, and `routes` data to resize the circles when zooming:

```
function zoomable(airports, R_scale, routes) {
  svg.call(
    d3.behavior.zoom()
      .translate(projection.translate())
      .scale(projection.scale())
      .on('zoom', function () {
              onzoom(airports, R_scale, routes);
      })
  );
}
```

We defined a zoom behavior with `d3.behavior.zoom()` and immediately called it on the whole image.

We set the current `.translate()` vector and `.scale()` to whatever the projection was using. The zoom event will call our `onzoom` function.

Let's define it:

```
function onzoom(airports, R_scale, routes) {
  projection
    .translate(d3.event.translate)
    .scale(d3.event.scale);

  d3.selectAll('path')
    .attr('d', d3.geo.path().projection(projection));
```

First we told our projection the new translation vector is in d3.event.translate. The translation vector will pan the map with a transformation, just like in *Chapter 2, A Primer on DOM, SVG, and CSS*. d3.event.scale is just a number the projection uses to scale itself, effectively zooming the map.

Then, we recalculated all the paths with a new d3.geo.path() using the changed projection.

```
d3.selectAll('circle')
    .attr('transform', function (id) {
        var airport = airports[id];
        return "translate("+projection([airport.lon, airport.
lat])+")";
    })
    .attr('r', function (id) {
      if (routes[id]) {
          var magnifier = d3.event.scale/1200;
          return magnifier*R_scale(routes[id].length);
      }else{
    return 1;
      }
    });
}
```

The same approach works for circles. Take the new info, select all the circles, and change their attributes.

The positioning function is exactly the same as in draw_airlines because geographic projections handle panning out of the box. Adjusting size takes a bit more work.

After calculating a magnifier as a ratio between the current and default scale (1200), we use R_scale to get the circle's normal size and multiply it by the magnifier.

You can now explore the world!

Have patience, though, it's slow. Redrawing everything on every move will do that.

For a more performant zoomable map, we'd have to use data with less detail when zoomed out, draw a sensible number of airports, and possibly avoid drawing parts of the map that fall out of the image anyway.

Brushes

Similar to zoom and drag, brushes are a simple way to create complex behavior — they enable users to select a part of the canvas.

Strangely enough, they aren't considered a behavior, but fall under the .svg namespace, perhaps because they are mostly meant for visual effects.

To create a new brush, we'd call d3.svg.brush() and define its x and y scales using .x() and .y(). We can also define a bounding rectangle.

Time for an example!

We're going to make a scatterplot of some random data and let the user select points. Begin with a drawing area and some data:

```
var width = 600,
    height = 600,
    svg = d3.select('#graph')
      .append('svg')
      .attr({width: width,
             height: height});

var random = d3.random.normal(.5, .11),
    data = d3.range(800).map(function (i) {
      return {x: random(),
              y: random()};
    });
```

We used a built-in random generator to create numbers with a `normal` distribution centered around `.5` and a dispersion of `.11`. d3.js also gives us the `logNormal` and `irwinHall` distributions.

We now have an array of 800 random two-dimensional positions. To draw them, we'll use two scales to make the tiny range more visible, then place each datum on the page as a circle.

```
var x = d3.scale.linear()
      .range([50, width-50]),
    y = d3.scale.linear()
      .range([height-50, 50]);

svg.append('g')
  .classed('circles', true)
  .selectAll('circle')
  .data(data)
  .enter()
  .append('circle')
  .attr({cx: function (d) { return x(d.x); },
         cy: function (d) { return y(d.y); },
         r: 4});
```

I know we don't usually add axes in this book, but scatterplots look ridiculous without them. Let's add some:

```
svg.append('g')
  .classed('axis', true)
```

```
      .attr('transform', 'translate(50, 0)')
      .call(d3.svg.axis().orient('left').scale(y));

  svg.append('g')
    .classed('axis', true)
    .attr('transform', 'translate(0, '+(height-50)+')')
    .call(d3.svg.axis().orient('bottom').scale(x));
```

You should remember what's going on here from *Chapter 2, A Primer on DOM, SVG, and CSS*, where we discussed axes at length.

Add some basic styling to the HTML:

```
<style>
  .axis path,
  .axis line {
    fill: none;
    stroke: black;
    shape-rendering: crispEdges;
  }
}
</style>
```

And yay, scatterplot!

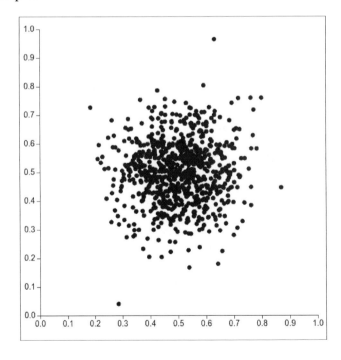

Now for the fun stuff:

```
svg.append("g")
  .classed("brush", true)
  .call(d3.svg.brush().x(x).y(y)
  .on("brushstart", brushstart)
  .on("brush", brushmove)
  .on("brushend", brushend));
```

We made a new grouping element for the brush and called a freshly constructed d3.svg.brush() with both scales defined. The "brush" class will help with styling. Finally, we defined listeners for brusthstart, brush, and brushend events.

```
function brushstart() {
  svg.select('.circles')
    .classed('selecting', true);
}
```

brushstart flicks the styling to selecting. We'll use it to help the user distinguish between selected and unselected circles:

```
function brushmove() {
  var e = d3.event.target.extent();

  svg.selectAll('circle')
    .classed("selected", function(d) {
        return e[0][0] <= d.x && d.x <= e[1][0]
        && e[0][1] <= d.y && d.y <= e[1][1];
    });
}
```

brushmove is where the real magic happens.

First, we find the selection's boundaries using d3.event.target.extent(). d3.event.target returns the current brush and .extent() returns a set of two points—upper-left and bottom-right corner.

Then, we go through all the circles and turn the selected class on or off, depending on whether a circle's position lies within the bounding box:

```
function brushend() {
  svg.select('.circles')
    .classed('selecting', !d3.event.target.empty());
}
```

brushend just turns off the selecting state if the selection is empty.

Our HTML needs some more styling definitions:

```
.brush .extent {
  stroke: #fff;
  fill-opacity: .125;
  shape-rendering: crispEdges;
}
circle {
  -webkit-transition: fill-opacity 125ms ease-in-out;
}
.selecting circle {
  fill-opacity: 0.25;
}
circle.selected {
  stroke: red;
}
```

We're changing the opacity of the circle fill (fill-opacity) rather than for the borders so that the circle edges always shine out at full opacity. Adding a CSS transition gives everything a smoother feel.

In this case, we prefer CSS transitions over what d3.js can do, so we can limit JavaScript to changing element states. Brushes sometimes also have problems with d3.js transitions and change properties immediately.

When you select some elements, the image will look like this:

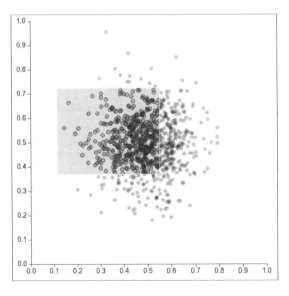

Summary

Wow, what a fun chapter!

You've made things jump around the page, almost killed your computer and patience with a zoomable map, and created a spinning thingy out of nothing but vertical lines.

This is everything you need for visualizations users can play with. The rest is just experimentation and some ingenuity in piecing things together. Good luck!

5
Layouts – d3's Black Magic

Most of us look at the Internet for inspiration and code samples. You find something that looks great, look at the code, and your eyes glaze over. It doesn't make any sense.

The usual culprit is d3's reliance on layouts for anything remotely complicated. The black magic of taking some data, calling a function, and voilà — visualization! This elegance makes layouts look deceptively difficult, but they make things a lot easier when you get a hang of them.

In this chapter, we'll go in, guns blazing, with everything we've learned so far to create 11 visualizations of the same dataset.

What are layouts and why should you care

d3 layouts are modules that transform data into drawing rules. The simplest layout might only transform an array of objects into coordinates, like a scale.

But we usually use layouts for more complex visualizations — drawing a force-directed graph or a tree, for instance. In these cases, layouts help us to separate calculating coordinates from putting pixels on a page. This not only makes our code cleaner, but it also lets us reuse the same layouts for vastly different visualizations.

Theory is boring, let's dig in.

Built-in layouts

By default, d3 comes with 12 built-in layouts that cover most common visualizations. They can be split roughly into normal and hierarchical layouts. The normal layouts are as follows:

- histogram
- pie
- stack
- chord
- force

The hierarchical layouts are as follows:

- partition
- tree
- cluster
- pack
- treemap

To see how they behave, we're going to make an example for each type. We'll start with the humble pie chart and histogram, then progress to force-directed graphs and fancy trees. We're using the same dataset for all examples, so that we can get a feel of how different presentations affect the perception of data.

These are the last examples in this book, so we're going to make them particularly magnificent. That's going to create a lot of code, so every time we come up with something reusable, we'll put it in a helpers.js file as a function.

Let's create an empty helper.js file:

```
window.helpers = {
};
```

We're going to add functions as members of this global object. Add the following line to the HTML right before including the normal code.

```
<script src="helpers.js"></script>
```

Let's also agree that all examples start with a drawing area and fetching the data.

```
var width = 1024,
    height = 1024,
    svg = d3.select('#graph')
```

```
        .append('svg')
        .attr({width: width,
              height: height});

    d3.json('data/karma_matrix.json', function (data) {
    });
```

Example code will go in the `d3.json` load listener.

The dataset

The dataset we'll be playing with has been scraped from my favorite IRC channel's log going back to late 2011. The channel's special feature is the karma bot.

When someone does something we like, we give them karma with `nick++` and the bot counts it as a vote for that person. Just like on Reddit, karma is supposed to measure how much the community likes someone, but it's really just about who is most active.

The karma is what we're interested in.

You can get the dataset at `https://raw.github.com/Swizec/d3.js-book-examples/master/ch5/data/karma_matrix.json`. The dataset consists of objects representing instances of giving karma. Each looks like the following code:

```
{"to": "smotko",
 "from": "Swizec",
 "time": "2012-02-28 23:44:40"}
```

Every object tells us at what time (`time`) somebody (`from`) gave karma to (`to`) somebody else. To deal with the cruft often tacked onto nicknames—for instance, `smotko` is `smotko-nexus` from his phone—only the first four letters of the nickname were considered when scraping the dataset.

This creates a clean dataset for us to work with. You can think of it as a list of edges in a graph, where users are nodes and `to` and `from` create a directed edge.

Time to draw!

Using the histogram layout

We are going to use the `histogram` layout to create a bar chart of the karma people have received. The layout itself will handle everything from collecting values into bins, to calculating heights, widths, and the positions of the bars.

Histograms usually represent a probability distribution over a continuous numerical domain, but nicknames are ordinal. To bend the `histogram` layout to our will, we have to turn nicknames into numbers—we'll use a scale.

Since it feels like this could be useful in other examples, we'll put the code in `helpers.js`:

```
uniques: function (data, nick) {
        var uniques = [];

        data.forEach(function (d) {
            if (uniques.indexOf(nick(d)) < 0) {
                uniques.push(nick(d));
            }
        });

        return uniques;
    },

    nick_id: function (data, nick) {
        var uniques = helpers.uniques(data, nick);

        return d3.scale.ordinal()
            .domain(uniques)
            .range(d3.range(uniques.length));
    },
```

These are two simple functions. `uniques` goes through the data and returns a list of unique nicknames. We help it with the `nick` accessor. `nick_id` creates an ordinal scale we'll be using to convert nicknames into numbers.

Now we can tell the histogram how to handle our data with `nick_id`.

```
var nick_id = helpers.nick_id(data, function (d) { return d.to; });

var histogram = d3.layout.histogram()
            .bins(nick_id.range())
            .value(function (d) { return nick_id(d.to); })(data);
```

Using `d3.layout.histogram()` we create a new histogram and use `.bins()` to define the upper threshold for each bin. Given [1,2,3], values under 1 go in the first bin, values between 1 and 2 in the second, and so on.

The `.value()` accessor tells the histogram how to find values in our dataset.

Another way to specify bins is by specifying the number of bins you want and letting the histogram uniformly divide a continuous numerical input domain into bins. For such domains, you can even make probability histograms by setting .frequency() to false. You can limit the range of considered bins with .range().

Finally, we used the layout as a function on our data to get an array of objects like this:

```
{0: {from: "HairyFotr",
        time: "2011-10-11 18:38:17",
        to: "notepad"},
    1: {from: "HairyFotr",
        time: "2012-01-09 10:41:53",
        to: "notepad"},
    dx: 1,
    x: 0,
    y: 2}
```

Bin width is in the dx property, x is the horizontal position and y is the height. We access elements in bins with normal array functions.

Using this data to draw a bar chart should be easy by now. We'll define a scale for each dimension, label both axes, and place some rectangles for bars.

To make things easier, we begin with some margins. Remember, all this code goes in the data load listener we defined earlier:

```
var margins = {top: 10,
                right: 40,
                bottom: 100,
                left: 50};
```

And two scales.

```
var x = d3.scale.linear()
            .domain([0, d3.max(histogram, function (d) { return d.x;
})])
            .range([margins.left, width-margins.right]),
        y = d3.scale.log()
            .domain([1, d3.max(histogram, function (d) { return d.y;
})])
            .range([height-margins.bottom, margins.top]);
```

Using a log scale for the vertical axis will make the graph easier to read despite the huge karma variations.

Next, put a vertical axis on the left:

```
var yAxis = d3.svg.axis()
            .scale(y)
            .tickFormat(d3.format('f'))
            .orient('left');

  svg.append('g')
      .classed('axis', true)
      .attr('transform', 'translate(50, 0)')
      .call(yAxis);
```

We create a grouping element for every bar and its label:

```
var bar = svg.selectAll('.bar')
            .data(histogram)
            .enter()
            .append('g')
            .classed('bar', true)
            .attr('transform',
                function (d) { return 'translate('+x(d.x)+',
'+y(d.y)+')'; });
```

Moving the group into position, as shown in the following code, means less work when positioning the bar and its label:

```
bar.append('rect')
        .attr({x: 1,
                width: x(histogram[0].dx)-margins.left-1,
                height: function (d) { return height-margins.bottom-
y(d.y); }
                });
```

Because the group is in place, we can put the bar a pixel from the group's edge. All bars will be `histogram[0].dx` wide and we'll calculate heights using the y position of each datum and the total graph height. Lastly, we create the labels:

```
bar.append('text')
        .text(function (d) { return d[0].to; })
        .attr({transform: function (d) {
                var bar_height = height-margins.bottom-y(d.y);

                return 'translate(0, '+(bar_height+7)+')
rotate(60)'; }
                });
```

We move labels to the bottom of the graph, rotate them by 60 degrees to avoid overlap, and set their text to the `.to` property of the datum.

Add some CSS styling to the HTML:

```
<style>
.axis path, .axis line {
  fill: none;
  stroke: #000;
  shape-rendering: crispEdges;
}

.axis text {
  font-size: 0.75em;
}

rect {
  fill: steelblue;
  shape-rendering: crispEdges;
}
</style>
```

Our bar chart looks like this:

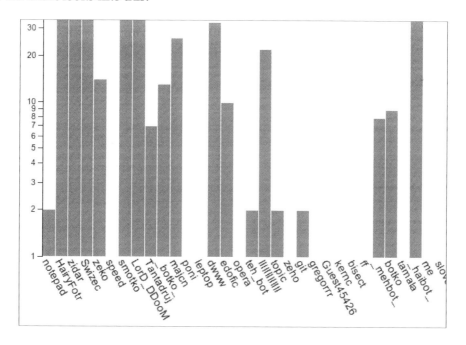

Well, the whole graph wouldn't fit in the book. Run the example.

Delicious pie

The previous bar chart reveals that **HairyFotr** has the most karma by far. Let's find out who's making him so popular.

We are going to use the pie chart layout to cut the karma of **HairyFotr** into slices, showing how much karma he gets from the others. After filtering the dataset for karma going to **HairyFotr**, we have to categorize entries by givers, and finally feed them into the pie chart layout to generate a pie chart.

We can use the `histogram` layout to put data into bins depending on the `.from` property. Let's add a function to `helpers.js`:

```
bin_per_nick: function (data, nick) {
    var nick_id = helpers.nick_id(data, nick);

    var histogram = d3.layout.histogram()
            .bins(nick_id.range())
            .value(function (d) { return nick_id(nick(d)); });

    histogram(data);

    return histogram;
},
```

Similar to the `uniques` and `nick_id` functions, `bin_per_nick` takes the data and a nick accessor, and returns histogram data.

We can now do this in pie chart's data listener:

```
filtered = data.filter(
        function (d) { return d.to == 'HairyFotr'; });

var per_nick = helpers.bin_per_nick(filtered,
                    function (d) { return d.from; });
```

Entries in the `per_nick` variable will tell us exactly how much karma **HairyFotr** got from someone.

To bake a pie, we call the `pie` layout and give it a value accessor:

```
var pie = d3.layout.pie()
        .value(function (d) { return d.length; })(per_nick);
```

The `pie` layout is now full of slice objects, each holding the `startAngle` and `endAngle` values and the original value.

Entries look like this:

```
{data: Array[135],
 endAngle: 2.718685950221936,
 startAngle: 0,
 value: 135}
```

We could have specified a `.sort()` function to change how slices are organized and a `.startAngle()` or `.endAngle()` function to limit the pie's size.

All that's left to do now is drawing a pie chart. We'll need an `arc` generator, just as the ones in *Chapter 2, A Primer on DOM, SVG*, and CSS and some color to tell slices apart.

Finding 24 distinct colors that look great together is hard; lucky for us, @ ponywithhiccups jumped to the challenge and made the pick. Thank you!

Let's add these colors to `helpers.js`:

```
color:  d3.scale.ordinal()
        .range(['#EF3B39', '#FFCD05', '#69C9CA', '#666699', '#CC3366',
'#0099CC',
                '#CCCB31', '#009966', '#C1272D', '#F79420', '#445CA9',
'#999999',
                '#402312', '#272361', '#A67C52', '#016735', '#F1AAAF',
'#FBF5A2',
                '#A0E6DA', '#C9A8E2', '#F190AC', '#7BD2EA', '#DBD6B6',
'#6FE4D0']),
```

The `color` scale is an ordinal scale without a domain. To make sure nicknames always get the same color, a function in `helpers.js` will help us fixate the domain, as shown in the following code:

```
fixate_colors: function (data) {
    helpers.color.domain(helpers.uniques(data,
                        function (d) { return d.from; }));
}
```

Now, we can define the `arc` generator and fixate the colors:

```
var arc = d3.svg.arc()
            .outerRadius(150)
            .startAngle(function (d) { return d.startAngle; })
            .endAngle(function (d) { return d.endAngle; });

helpers.fixate_colors(data);
```

A group element will hold each arc and its label as shown in the following code:

```
var slice = svg.selectAll('.slice')
            .data(pie)
            .enter()
            .append('g')
            .attr('transform', 'translate(300, 300)');
```

To make positioning simpler, we move every group to the center of the pie chart. Creating slices works the same as in *Chapter 2, A Primer on DOM, SVG, and CSS*:

```
slice.append('path')
        .attr({d: arc,
                fill: function (d) { return colors(d.data[0].from);
}
            });
```

We get the color for a slice with `d.data[0].from`—the original dataset is in `.data` and all the `.from` properties in it are the same. That's what we grouped by.

Labels take a bit more work. They need to be rotated into place and sometimes flipped so that they don't appear upside-down.

Labeling an arc will be handy later as well, so let's make a general function in `helpers.js`:

```
arc_labels: function (text, radius) {
        return function (selection) {
            selection.append('text')
                .text(text)
                .attr('text-anchor', function (d) {
                    return helpers.tickAngle(d) > 100 ? 'end' :
'start';
                })
                .attr('transform', function (d) {
                    var degrees = helpers.tickAngle(d);

                    var turn = 'rotate('+degrees+')
translate('+(radius(d)+10)+', 0)';

                    if (degrees > 100) {
```

```
                                turn += 'rotate(180)';
                    }

                    return turn;
                });
        }
    },
```

We're using partial application to generate a function operating on a d3 selection. This means we can use it with `.call()`, while still defining our own parameters.

We'll give `arc_labels` a `text` accessor and a `radius` accessor, and it will return a function we can use with `.call()` on a selection to make labels appear in just the right places. The meaty part appends a text element, tweaks its `text-anchor` element, depending on whether we're going to flip it, and rotates the element into a particular position with the help of a `tickAngle` function.

Let's add the contents of the `tickAngle` function:

```
tickAngle: function (d) {
        var midAngle = (d.endAngle-d.startAngle)/2,
            degrees = (midAngle+d.startAngle)/Math.PI*180-90;

        return degrees;
    }
```

`helpers.tickAngle` calculates the middle angle between `d.startAngle` and `d.endAngle` and transforms the result from radians to degrees so that SVG can understand it.

This is basic trigonometry, so I won't go into details, but your favorite high schooler should be able to explain the math.

We use `arc_labels` back in the load listener:

```
slice.call(helpers.arc_labels(
                    function (d) { return d.data[0].from; },
                    arc.outerRadius()));
```

And our delicious pie is done as shown in the following screenshot:

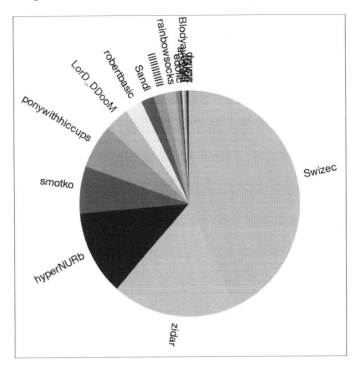

Clearly, the smallest values could do with some grouping under other, but you can play around with that on your own.

Showing popularity through time with stack

D3's official docs say:

> *"The stack layout takes a two-dimensional array of data and computes a baseline; the baseline is then propagated to the above layers, so as to produce a stacked graph."*

Not clear at all, but I am hard pressed to come up with better. The `stack` layout calculates where one layer ends and another begins. An example should help.

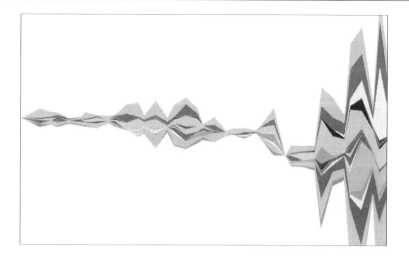

We're going to make a layered timeline of karma, stretching as far back as 2011, with the width of each layer telling us how much karma went to a user at a certain time. This timeline is called a **streamgraph**.

To label layers, we're going to create a `mouseover` behavior that highlights a layer and shows a tooltip with the user's nickname. By fiddling until the graph looked pretty, I discovered that we should bin data into 12-day slots.

Let's begin the binning:

```
var time = d3.time.format('%Y-%m-%d %H:%M:%S'),
        extent = d3.extent(data.map(function (d) { return time.
parse(d.time); })),
        time_bins = d3.time.days(extent[0], extent[1], 12);
```

To parse timestamps into date objects, we specified a format for strings like `2012-01-25 15:32:15`. Then, we used this format to find the earliest and latest time with `d3.extent`. Telling `d3.time.days()` to go from start to finish with a step of 12 days creates a list of bins.

We use the `histogram` layout to munge our dataset into a more useful form:

```
var per_nick = helpers.bin_per_nick(data, function (d) { return d.to;
});

    var time_binned  = per_nick.map(function (nick_layer) {
        return {to: nick_layer[0].to,
```

```
            values: d3.layout.histogram()
                        .bins(time_bins)
                        .value(function (d) {
                                return time.parse(d.time);
}) (nick_layer)};
    });
```

You already know what `helpers.bin_per_nick` does.

To bin data into time slots, we mapped through each layer of the `nick` accessors and turned it into a two-property object. The `.to` property tells us whom the layer represents, and `.values` is a histogram of time slots where entries tell us how much karma the user got in a certain 12-day period.

Time for a `stack` layout:

```
var layers = d3.layout.stack()
        .order('inside-out')
        .offset('wiggle')
        .values(function (d) { return d.values; }) (time_binned);
```

`d3.layout.stack()` creates a new `stack` layout. We told it how to order layers with `.order('inside-out')` (you should also try `default` and `reverse`) and decided how the final graph looks with `.offset('wiggle')`. `wiggle` minimizes change in slope. Other options include `silhouette`, `zero`, and `expand`. Try them.

Once again, we told the layout how to find values with the `.values()` accessor.

Our `layers` array is now filled with objects like this:

```
{to: "notepad",
    values: Array[50]}
```

`values` is an array of arrays. Entries in the outer array are time bins that look like this:

```
{dx: 1036800000,
    length: 1,
    x: Object(Thu Oct 13 2011 00:00:00 GMT+0200 (CEST)),
    y: 1,
    y0: 140.16810522517937}
```

The important parts of this array are as follows:

`x` is the horizontal position, `y` is the thickness, and `y0` is the baseline. `d3.layout.stack` will always return these.

To start drawing, we need some margins and two scales:

```
var margins = {
        top: 220,
        right: 50,
        bottom: 0,
        left: 50
    };

var x = d3.time.scale()
            .domain(extent)
            .range([margins.left, width-margins.right]),
    y = d3.scale.linear()
            .domain([0, d3.max(layers, function (layer) {
                return d3.max(layer.values, function (d) {
                    return d.y0+d.y;
                });
            })])
            .range([height-margins.top, 0]);
```

The tricky thing was finding the vertical scale's domain. We found it by going through each value of every layer, looking for the maximum d.y0+d.y value — baseline plus thickness.

We'll use an area path generator for the layers;

```
var offset = 100,
    area = d3.svg.area()
            .x(function(d) { return x(d.x); })
            .y0(function(d) { return y(d.y0)+offset; })
            .y1(function(d) { return y(d.y0 + d.y)+offset; });
```

Nothing too fancy, the baselines define bottom edges and adding the thickness gives the top edge. Fiddling determined that both should be pushed down by 100 pixels.

Let's draw an axis first:

```
var xAxis = d3.svg.axis()
            .scale(x)
            .tickFormat(d3.time.format('%b %Y'))
            .ticks(d3.time.months, 2)
            .orient('bottom');

svg.append('g')
    .attr('transform', 'translate(0, '+(height-100)+')')
    .classed('axis', true)
    .call(xAxis);
```

Same as usual—we defined an axis, called it on a selection, and let d3 do its thing. We only made it prettier with a custom `.tickFormat()` function and used `.ticks()` to say we want a new tick every two months.

Ok, now for the streamgraph, add the following code:

```
svg.selectAll('path')
        .data(layers)
        .enter()
        .append('path')
        .attr('d', function (d) { return area(d.values); })
        .style('fill', function (d, i) { return helpers.color(i); })
        .call(helpers.tooltip(function (d) { return d.nick; });
```

Not much is going on. We used the `area` generator to draw each layer, defined colors with `helpers.color`, and called a `tooltip` function, which we'll define in `helpers.js` later.

The graph looks like this:

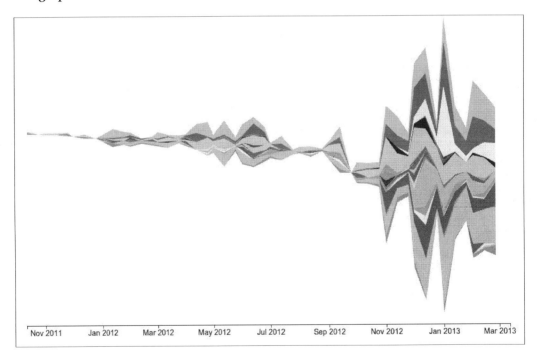

It looks pretty, but it is useless. Let's add that `tooltip` function to `helpers.js`:

```
tooltip: function (text) {
        return function (selection) {
```

```
selection.on('mouseover.tooltip', mouseover)
    .on('mousemove.tooltip', mousemove)
    .on('mouseout.tooltip', mouseout);
}
}
```

We defined event listeners with a `.tooltip` namespace so that we can define multiple listeners on the same events.

The `mouseover` function will highlight streams and create tooltips, `mousemove` will move tooltips, and `mouseout` will put everything back to normal.

Let's put the three listeners inside the inner function:

```
function mouseover(d) {
    var path = d3.select(this);
     path.classed('highlighted', true);
}
```

That's the simple part of `mouseover`. It selects the current area and changes its class to `highlighted`. That will make it lighter and add a red outline.

In the same function, add the meaty part:

```
var mouse = d3.mouse(svg.node());
    var tool = svg.append('g')
            .attr({'id': "nicktool",
                transform: 'translate('+(mouse[0]+5)+',
'+(mouse[1]+10)+')'});

    var textNode = tool.append('text')
                    .text(text(d)).node();

    tool.append('rect')
        .attr({height: textNode.getBBox().height,
            width: textNode.getBBox().width,
            transform: 'translate(0, -16)'});

    tool.select('text')
        .remove();

    tool.append('text')
        .text(d.nick);
```

It is longer and with a dash of magic, but not scary at all!

First we find the mouse's position, then create a group element, and position it down and to the right of the mouse. We add a text element to the group and call SVG's `getBBox()` function on its node. This gives us the text element's bounding box and helps us size the background rectangle.

Finally, we remove the text because it's covered by the background and add it again. We might be able to avoid all this trouble by using divs, but I wanted to show you pure SVG tooltips. Hence, consider the following code:

```
function mousemove () {
    var mouse = d3.mouse(svg.node());
    d3.select('#nicktool')
        .attr('transform', 'translate('+(mouse[0]+15)+',
'+(mouse[1]+20)+')');
}
```

The `mousemove` listener in the following code is much simpler. It just finds the `#nicktool` element and moves it to follow the cursor.

```
function mouseout () {
    var path = d3.select(this);
    path.classed('highlighted', false);

    d3.select('#nicktool').remove();
}
```

The `mouseout` function selects the current path, removes its `highlighted` styling, and removes the tooltip.

Voila! Tooltips

Very rudimentary — they don't understand edges and they won't break any hearts with their looks, but they get the job done. Let's add some CSS to the HTML:

```
<style>
.axis path, .axis line {
  fill: none;
  stroke: #000;
  shape-rendering: crispEdges;
}

path.highlighted {
  fill-opacity: 0.5;
  stroke: red;
  stroke-width: 1.5;
}
```

```
#nicktool {
   font-size: 1.3em;
}

#nicktool rect {
   fill: white;
}
</style>
```

And now we have a potentially useful streamgraph on our hands.

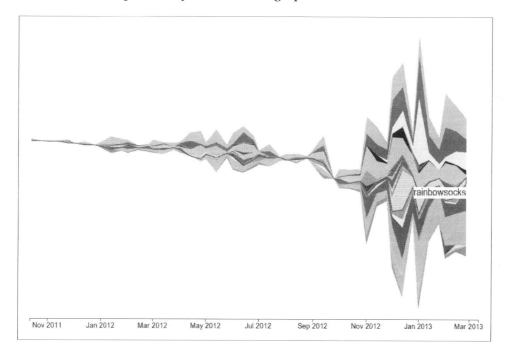

Highlighting friends with chord

We've seen how much karma people have and when they got it, but there's another gem hiding in the data — connections. We can visualize who is a friend of whom using the `chord` layout.

We're going to draw a chord diagram — a circular diagram of connections between users. Chord diagrams are often used in genetics and have even appeared on covers of magazines (`http://circos.ca/intro/published_images/`).

Ours is going to have an outer ring showing how much karma users give out and chords showing where that karma is going.

First, we need a matrix of connections for the chord diagram, and then we'll go the familiar route of path generators and adding elements. The matrix code will be useful later, so let's put it in `helpers.js`:

```
connection_matrix: function (data) {
        var nick_id = helpers.nick_id(data, function (d) { return
d.from; }),
            uniques = nick_id.domain();

        var matrix = d3.range(uniques.length).map(function () {
            return d3.range(uniques.length).map(function () { return
0; });
        });

        data.forEach(function (d) {
            matrix[nick_id(d.from)][nick_id(d.to)] += 1;
        });

        return matrix;
    }
```

We begin with the familiar `uniques` list and the `nick_id` scale, then create a zero matrix, and loop through the data to increase connection counts in cells. Rows are *from whom*, columns are *to whom* — if the fifth cell in the first row holds `10`, the first user has given ten karma to the fifth user. This is called an **adjacency matrix**.

Back in the load listener, we can do this:

```
    var uniques = helpers.uniques(data, function (d) { return d.from;
}),
        matrix = helpers.connection_matrix(data);
```

We're going to need `uniques` for labels and it would be nice to have the `innerRadius` and `outerRadius` variables handy:

```
var innerRadius = Math.min(width, height)*0.3,
        outerRadius = innerRadius*1.1;
```

Time to make the `chord` layout do our bidding:

```
var chord = d3.layout.chord()
                .padding(.05)
                .sortGroups(d3.descending)
                .sortSubgroups(d3.descending)
                .sortChords(d3.descending)
                .matrix(matrix);
```

It is a little different from others. The `chord` layout takes data via the `.matrix()` method and can't be called as a function.

We started with `d3.layout.chord()` and put some `.padding()` method between groups which improves readability. To improve readability further, everything is sorted. `.sortGroups` sorts groups on the edge, `.sortSubgroups` sorts chord attachments in groups, and `.sortChords` sorts chord drawing order so that smaller chords overlap bigger ones.

In the end, we feed data into the layout with `.matrix()`:

```
var diagram = svg.append('g')
            .attr('transform', 'translate('+width/2+','+height/2+')');
```

We add a centered group element so that all our coordinates are relative to the center from now on.

Drawing the diagram happens in three steps—arcs, labels, and chords, as shown in the following code:

```
var group = diagram.selectAll('.group')
            .data(chord.groups)
            .enter()
            .append('g'),
    arc = d3.svg.arc()
                .innerRadius(innerRadius)
                .outerRadius(outerRadius);

group.append('path')
    .attr('d', arc)R
    .attr('fill', function (d) {
        return helpers.color(d.index); });
```

This creates the outer ring. We used `chord.groups` to get group data from the layout, created a new grouping element for every chord group, and then added an arc. We use `arc_labels` from the pie example to add the labels:

```
group.call(helpers.arc_labels(
        function (d) { return uniques[d.index]; },
        function () { return outerRadius+10; }));
```

Even though the radius is constant, we have to define it as a function using the following code because we didn't make `arc_labels` flexible enough for constants. Shame on us!

```
diagram.append('g')
        .classed('chord', true)
        .selectAll('path')
        .data(chord.chords)
```

```
        .enter()
        .append('path')
        .attr('d', d3.svg.chord().radius(innerRadius))
        .attr('fill', function (d, i) { return helpers.color(d.target.
index); });
```

We got chord data from `chord.chords` and used a `chord path` generator to draw the chords. We pick colors with `d.target.index` because the graph looks better, but chord colors are *not* informative.

We add some CSS to make chords easier to follow:

```
<style>
.chord path {
   stroke: black;
   stroke-width: 0.2;
   opacity: 0.6;
}
</style>
```

And our diagram looks perfect:

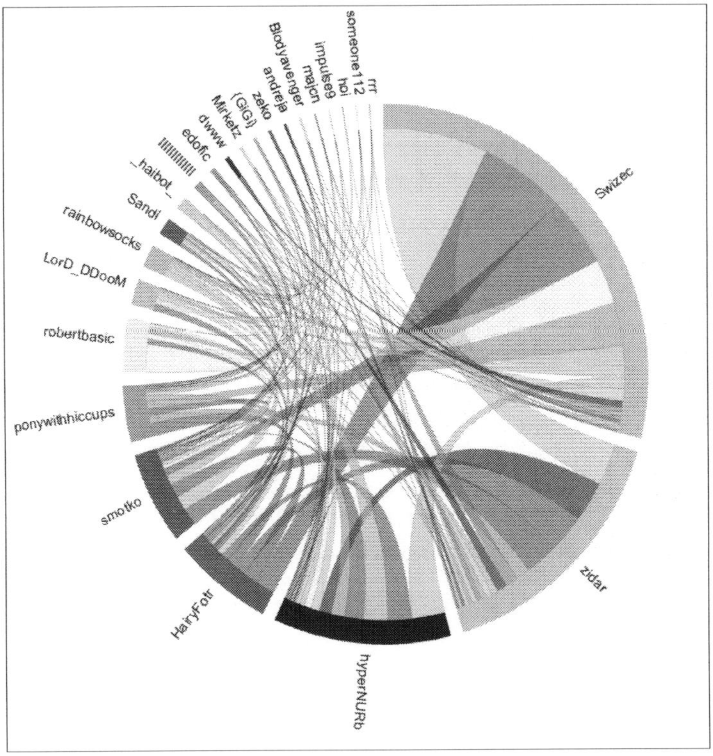

It looks pretty but unintuitive. We spent hours bickering on IRC before we figured it out.

First of all, chord colors don't mean anything! They just make it easier to distinguish chords. Furthermore, this graph shows how much karma everyone is *giving*.

From my arc's size you can see I've given about 30 percent of the karma ever given on this channel. I might be too generous.

The width of chords touching my arc tells you how much of that karma is going to whom.

At the other end of each chord, it's exactly the same. Chord width tells you how much karma that user has given me. Chords are bidirectional connections between users.

Drawing with force

The `force` layout is the most complicated of the non-hierarchical layouts. It lets you draw complex graphs using physical simulations—force-directed graphs if you will. Everything you draw will have built-in animation.

We're going to draw a graph of connections between users. Every user will be a node, the size of which will correspond to the user's karma. Links between nodes will tell us who is giving karma to whom.

To make things clearer, we're going to add tooltips and make sure mousing over a node highlights the connected nodes.

Let's begin.

As in the chord example, we begin with a matrix of connections. We aren't going to feed this directly to the `force` layout, but we will use it to create the kind of data it enjoys:

```
var nick_id = helpers.nick_id(data, function (d) { return d.from; }),
    uniques = nick_id.domain(),
    matrix = helpers.connection_matrix(data);
```

The `force` layout expects an array of nodes and links. Let's make them:

```
var nodes = uniques.map(function (nick) {
    return {nick: nick};
});
var links = data.map(function (d) {
```

```
         return {source: nick_id(d.from),
                  target: nick_id(d.to),
                  count: matrix[nick_id(d.from)][nick_id(d.to)]};
      });
```

We're defining the bare minimum of what we need, and the layout will calculate all the hard stuff.

nodes tell us who they represent and links connect a source object to a target object with an index into the nodes array—the layout will turn them into proper references as shown in the following code. Every link also contains a count object that we'll use to define its strength.

```
var force = d3.layout.force()
            .nodes(nodes)
            .links(links)
            .gravity(0.5)
            .size([width, height]);


   force.start();
```

We create a new force layout with d3.layout.force(); just like the chord layout, it isn't a function either. We feed in the data with .nodes() and .links().

Gravity pulls the graph towards the center of the image; we defined its strength with .gravity(). We tell the force layout the size of our picture with .size().

No calculation happens until force.start() is called, but we need the results to define a few scales for later.

There are a few more parameters to play with: overall .friction() (the smallest .linkDistance() value the nodes stabilize to), .linkStrength() for link stretchiness, and .charge() for attraction between nodes. Play with them.

nodes members look like this now:

```
{index: 0,
  nick: "HairyFotr",
  px: 497.0100389553633,
  py: 633.2734045531992,
  weight: 458,
  x: 499.5873097327753,
  y: 633.395804766377}
```

weight tells us how many links connect with this node, px and py are its previous
positions, and x and y are the current position.

links members are a lot simpler:

```
{count: 2
   source: Object
   target: Object}
```

Both source and target objects are a direct reference to the correct node.

Now that the layout made its first calculation step, we have the data to define
some scales;

```
var weight = d3.scale.linear()
        .domain(d3.extent(nodes.map(function (d) { return
d.weight; })))
        .range([5, 30]),
    distance = d3.scale.linear()
        .domain(d3.extent(d3.merge(matrix)))
        .range([300, 100]),
    given = d3.scale.linear()
        .range([2, 35]);
```

We're going to use the weight scale for node sizes, distance for link lengths,
and given to scale nodes for the highlighting effect:

```
force.linkDistance(function (d) {
        return distance(d.count);
    });

force.start();
```

We use .linkDistance() to dynamically define link lengths according
to the .count property. To put the change in effect, we restart the layout
with force.start().

Finally! Time to put some ink on paper—well, pixels on screen:

```
var link = svg.selectAll("line")
            .data(links)
            .enter()
            .append("line")
            .classed('link', true);
```

Links are simple—go through the list of links and draw a `line`.

Draw a circle for every node and give it the right size and color. The strange `nick_` class will help us with the highlighting we're doing in the two mouse event listeners:

```
var node = svg.selectAll("circle")
              .data(nodes)
              .enter()
              .append("circle")
              .classed('node', true)
              .attr({r: function (d) { return weight(d.weight); },
                     fill: function (d) { return helpers.color(d.index);
},
                     class: function (d) { return 'nick_'+nick_id(d.
nick); }})
              .on('mouseover', function (d) {
                  highlight(d, uniques, given, matrix, nick_id);
              })
              .on('mouseout', function (d) {
                  dehighlight(d, weight);
              });
```

We add tooltips with the familiar `helpers.tooltip` function and `force.drag` will automatically make the nodes draggable:

```
node.call(helpers.tooltip(function (d) { return d.nick; }));
node.call(force.drag);
```

After all that work, we still have to do the updating on every tick of the `force` layout animation:

```
force.on("tick", function() {
      link.attr("x1", function(d) { return d.source.x; })
          .attr("y1", function(d) { return d.source.y; })
          .attr("x2", function(d) { return d.target.x; })
          .attr("y2", function(d) { return d.target.y; });

      node.attr("cx", function(d) { return d.x; })
          .attr("cy", function(d) { return d.y; });
   });
```

On a `tick` event, we move every `link` endpoint and `node` to its new position. Simple.

Time to define the two highlighting functions we mentioned earlier:

```
function highlight (d, uniques, given, matrix, nick_id) {
    given.domain(d3.extent(matrix[nick_id(d.nick)]));

    uniques.map(function (nick) {
        var count = matrix[nick_id(d.nick)][nick_id(nick)];

        if (nick != d.nick) {
            d3.selectAll('circle.nick_'+nick_id(nick))
                .classed('unconnected', true)
                .transition()
                .attr('r', given(count));
        }
    });
}
```

The `highlight` function will grow all connected nodes according to how much karma they've gotten from the node we're touching with the mouse. It starts by setting the `given` object's domain, then goes through the `uniques` list, resizes corresponding nodes using the `given` scale for size, and uses `nick_id` to find the nodes.

The current node is left alone.

`dehighlight` will remove all the shenanigans we caused:

```
function mouseout (d, weight) {
    d3.selectAll('.node')
        .transition()
        .attr('r', function (d) { return weight(d.weight); });
}
```

Add some styling to the HTML:

```
<style>
line {
  stroke: lightgrey;
  stroke-width: 0.3;
}

#nicktool {
  font-size: 1.3em;
}
</style>
```

And voilà! We get a force-directed graph of user connections.

Running this example looks silly because it spins around a lot before settling down. But once it stabilizes, the graph looks something like this:

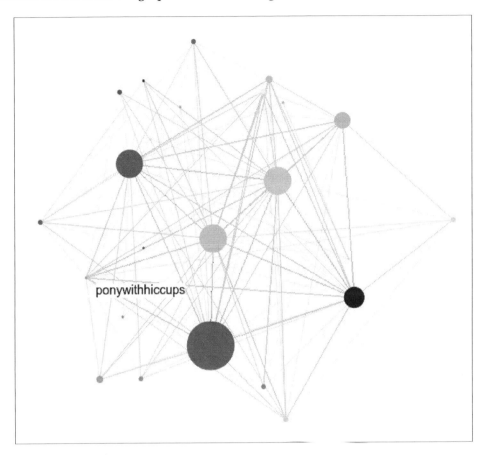

The graph would be more interesting if all nodes were not connected, but hovering one of the smaller nodes will reveal interesting connections.

We should have added some code to print names next to the highlighted nodes, but the example was long enough. Let's say that's left as an exercise for the reader.

We will now move towards hierarchical layouts!

Hierarchical layouts

All hierarchical layouts are based on an abstract hierarchy layout designed for representing hierarchical data — data within data within data within data within.... You get the idea.

All the common code for the `partition`, `tree`, `cluster`, `pack`, and `treemap` layouts is defined in `d3.layout.hierarchy()` and they all follow similar design patterns. The layouts are so similar that the official documentation very obviously copy-pastes most of its explanations. Let's avoid that by looking at the common stuff first, and then we will focus on the differences.

First of all, we need some hierarchical data. I spent an afternoon trying to make our karma dataset hierarchical. The result was a scheme that works well with three of the layouts and looks contrived for the other two. Sorry about that.

It's simple really, we kill the Batman.

We'll have a root node called `karma`, which will contain the 24 users who have ever given karma. For the `tree` and `cluster` layouts, each of those will contain nodes for everyone they have given karma to. For the `partition`, `pack`, and `treemap` layouts, children nodes will tell us who contributed to the parent's karma.

The final data structure will look like this:

```
{
    "nick": "karma",
    "children": [
        {
            "nick": "HairyFotr",
            "count": 312,
            "children": [
                {
                    "nick": "notepad",
                    "count": 2,
                    "children": []
                },
                {
                    "nick": "LorD_DDooM",
                    "count": 6,
                    "children": []
                },
```

While it could potentially go on forever, that wouldn't make sense in our case.

The default accessor expects a `.children` property, but we could easily have done something crazy like dynamically generating a fractal structure in a custom accessor.

As usual, there's a `.value()` accessor that helps layouts to find data in a node. We'll use it for the `.count` property—to check how much karma a user's got.

To run a hierarchical layout, we call `.nodes()` with our dataset. This immediately returns a list of nodes that you can't get to later. For a list of connections, we call `.links()` with a list of our nodes. Nodes in the returned list will have some extra properties calculated by the layout. Most layouts tell us where to put something with `.x` and `.y`, then use `.dx` and `.dy` to tell us how big the layout should be.

All hierarchical layouts also support sorting with `.sort()`, which takes a sorting function such as `d3.ascending` or `d3.descending`.

Enough theory, let's add a data munging function to `helpers.js`:

```
make_tree: function (data, filter1, filter2, nick1, nick2) {
        var tree = {nick: 'karma',
                    children: []};
        var uniques = helpers.uniques(data, function (d) { return
d.from; });

        tree.children = uniques.map(
            function (nick) {
                var my_karma = data.filter(function (d) { return
filter1(d, nick); }).length,
                    given_to = helpers.bin_per_nick(
                        data.filter(function (d) { return filter2(d,
nick); }),
                        nick1
                );

                return {nick: nick,
                        count: my_karma,
                        children: given_to.map(function (d) {
                            return {nick: nick2(d),
                                    count: d.length,
                                    children: []};
                        })};
            });

        return tree;
    },
```

Wow, there's a lot going on here. We avoided recursion because we know our data will never nest more than two levels deep.

`tree` holds an empty root node at first. We use `helpers.uniques` to get a list of nicknames, then map through the array and define the children of the root node by counting everyone's karma and using `helpers.bin_per_nick` to get an array of children.

The code is wibbly-wobbly because we use `filter1`, `filter2`, `nick1`, and `nick2` for data accessors, but making this function flexible makes it useful in all hierarchical examples.

Drawing a tree

The `tree` layout displays data in a tree using the tidy **Reingold-Tilford** tidy algorithm. We'll use it to display our dataset in a large circular tree with every node connected to its parent by a curvy line.

We begin the load listener by fixating colors, turning data into a tree, and defining a way to draw curvy lines:

```
helpers.fixate_colors(data);

var tree = helpers.make_tree(data,
                  function (d, nick) { return d.to == nick; },
                  function (d, nick) { return d.from == nick; },
                  function (d) { return d.to; },
                  function (d) { return d[0].to; });

var diagonal = d3.svg.diagonal.radial()
        .projection(function(d) { return [d.y, d.x / 180 * Math.PI]; });
```

You know `fixate_colors` from before, we defined `make_tree` not a page ago, and we've talked about the `diagonal` generator in *Chapter 2, A Primer on DOM, SVG, and CSS.*

```
var layout = d3.layout.tree()
            .size([360, width/2 - 120]);

    var nodes = layout.nodes(tree),
        links = layout.links(nodes);
```

We create a new tree layout by calling `d3.layout.tree()`. Defining its size with `.size()` and executing it with `.nodes()`. `.size()` tells the layout how much room it's got—in this case, we're using `x` as an angle (360 degrees) and `y` as a radius. Though the layout itself doesn't really care about that.

To avoid worrying about centering later on, we put a grouping element center stage:

```
var chart = svg.append('g')
              .attr('transform', 'translate('+width/2+','+height/2+')');
```

First we are going to draw the links, then the nodes and their labels:

```
var link = chart.selectAll(".link")
            .data(links)
            .enter()
            .append("path")
            .attr("class", "link")
            .attr("d", diagonal);
```

You should be familiar with this by now; go through the data and append new paths shaped with the `diagonal` generator:

```
var node = chart.selectAll(".node")
            .data(nodes)
            .enter().append("g")
            .attr("class", "node")
            .attr("transform", function(d) { return "rotate(" + (d.x -
90) + ")translate(" + d.y + ")"; });
```

For every node in the data, we create a new grouping element and move it into place using `rotate` for angles and `translate` for radius positions.

Now it's just a matter of adding a circle and a label:

```
node.append("circle")
    .attr("r", 4.5)
    .attr('fill', function (d) { return helpers.color(d.nick); });

node.append("text")
    .attr("dy", ".31em")
    .attr("text-anchor", function(d) { return d.x < 180 ? "start"
: "end"; })
    .attr("transform", function(d) { return d.x < 180 ?
"translate(8)" : "rotate(180)translate(-8)"; })
    .text(function(d) { return d.nick; })
    .style('font-size', function (d) { return d.depth > 1 ?
'0.8em' : '1.1em'; });
```

Every node is colored with the user's native color and the text is transformed similarly to the earlier pie and chord examples. Finally, we made leaf nodes' text smaller to avoid overlap.

After this, we will add some styling:

```
<style>
.link {
  fill: none;
  stroke: lightgrey;
}
</style>
```

Our tree looks like this:

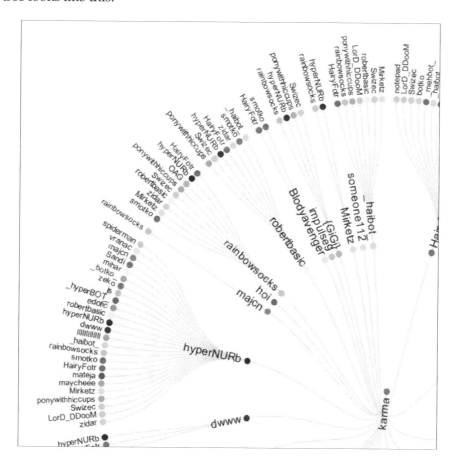

It's rather big, so you should try it out in the browser. Just remember, the inner ring is users giving karma to the outer ring.

Showing clusters

The `cluster` layout is the same as the `tree` layout, except that leaf nodes line up.

Do you see that the **hoi** user is hanging out in the inner ring of the tree example? With the cluster layout they end up on the outside with the other leaf nodes.

Codewise this example is the same as the last, so we won't go through it again. Really, the only difference is that we don't have to flip labels at certain angles. You can look at the code on the GitHub examples repository `https://github.com/Swizec/d3.js-book-examples/blob/master/ch5/cluster.js`.

We end up with a very tall graph that looks something like this:

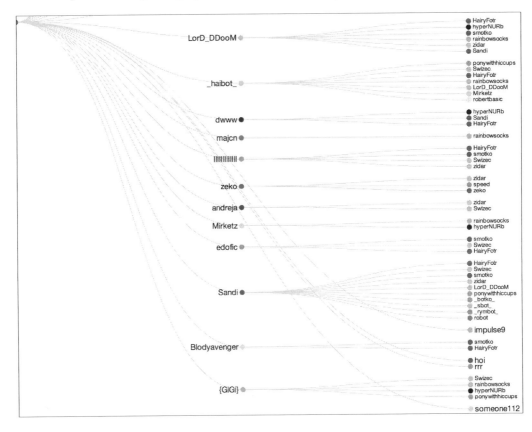

Partitioning a pie

Now we're getting somewhere! The next three layouts fit our data perfectly — we're taking three looks at how our core users' karma is structured.

The partition layout creates adjacency diagrams, where you don't draw nodes with links between them, but next to each other so that it looks like the children partition the parent.

We are going to draw a two-layer donut chart. Users will go on the first layer and the layer on top will show us where the karma is coming from.

We begin by munging the dataset and fixating colors:

```
var tree = helpers.make_tree(data,
                function (d, nick) { return d.to == nick; },
                function (d, nick) { return d.to == nick; },
                function (d) { return d.from; },
                function (d) { return d[0].from; });
helpers.fixate_colors(data);
```

Then use the partition layout:

```
var partition = d3.layout.partition()
        .value(function (d) { return d.count; })
        .sort(function (a, b) {
            return d3.descending(a.count, b.count);
        })
        .size([2*Math.PI, 300]);

var nodes = partition.nodes(tree);
```

We used .value() to tell the layout we care about the .count values, and we'll get a better picture if we .sort() the output. Similarly, to the tree layout, x will represent angles — this time in radians — and y will be radii.

We need an arc generator as well, as shown in the following code:

```
var arc = d3.svg.arc()
        .innerRadius(function (d) { return d.y; })
        .outerRadius(function (d) {
                            return d.depth ? d.y+d.dy/d.depth :
  0; });
```

The generator will use each node's `.y` property for the inner radius and add `.dy` for the outer radius. Fiddling shows the outer layer should be thinner, hence we are dividing it by the tree depth.

Notice that there's no accessor for `.startAngle` and `.endAngle`, which are stored as `.x` and `.dx`. It's easier to just fix the data:

```
nodes = nodes.map(function (d) {
    d.startAngle = d.x;
    d.endAngle = d.x+d.dx;
    return d;
});


nodes = nodes.filter(function (d) { return d.depth; });
```

It is as simple as mapping the data and defining angle properties, then filtering the data to make sure the root isn't drawn.

We use the familiar grouping trick to center our diagram.

```
var chart = svg.append('g')
        .attr('transform', 'translate('+width/2+','+height/2+')');
```

Preparation work is done. It's drawing time:

```
var node = chart.selectAll('g')
        .data(nodes)
        .enter()
        .append('g');

node.append('path')
    .attr({d: arc,
           fill: function (d) { return helpers.color(d.nick); }});
```

An arc is drawn for every node, color is chosen as usual:

```
node.filter(function (d) { return d.depth > 1 && d.count > 10; })
    .call(helpers.arc_labels(function (d) { return d.nick; },
                             arc.outerRadius()));

node.call(helpers.tooltip(function (d) { return d.nick; }));
```

We add labels and tooltips with the functions prepared in earlier examples. We avoid adding labels for very thin slices so that they don't overlap and make a mess. Sprinkle some CSS:

```
<style>
path {
  stroke: white;
  stroke-width: 2;
}

#nicktool {
  font-size: 1.3em;
}

#nicktool rect {
  fill: white;
}
</style>
```

The adjacency diagram looks like this:

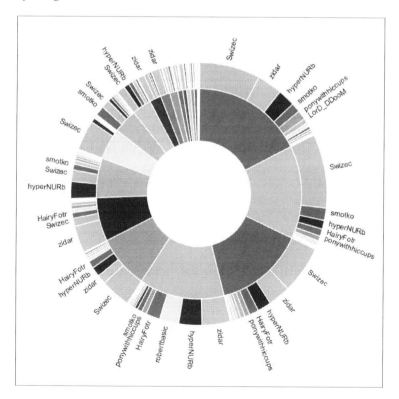

Packing circles into circles

The `pack` layout uses packing to visually represent hierarchies. It stuffs children nodes into their parents, trying to conserve space and sizing each node so that it's the cumulative size of its children.

Conceptually it's very similar to the `treemap` layout, so I'm going to skip all the code and just show you the picture. You can still see the code over at GitHub `https://github.com/Swizec/d3.js-book-examples/blob/master/ch5/pack.js`.

 The code is rather familiar—generate a tree, fixate colors, create layout, tweak a few parameters, get computed nodes, draw nodes, and add tooltips. Simple.

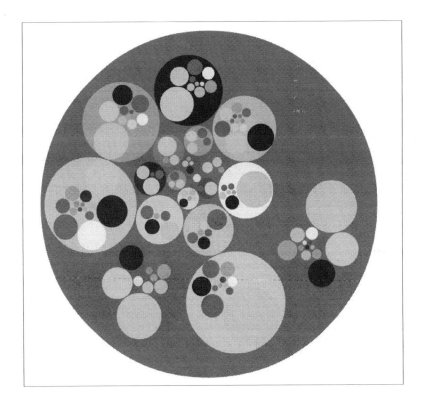

It looks very pretty, but not too informative. Adding labels wouldn't help much because most nodes are too small.

Subdividing with treemap

The `treemap` layout subdivides nodes with horizontal and vertical slices, essentially packing children into their parents just like the `pack` layout, but using rectangles. As a result, node sizes on every level can be compared directly, making this one of the best layouts for analyzing cumulative effects of subdivisions.

We are going to have some fun with this example. Tooltips will name the parent—parents are almost completely obscured by the children—and mousing over a node will make unrelated nodes become lighter, making the graph less confusing (at least in theory).

It's also a cool effect and a great way to end this chapter on layouts.

We begin with the boring stuff; prepare data and fixate colors:

```
var tree = helpers.make_tree(data,
              function (d, nick) { return d.to == nick; },
              function (d, nick) { return d.to == nick; },
              function (d) { return d.from; },
              function (d) { return d[0].from; });
helpers.fixate_colors(data);
```

Creating the `treemap` layout follows familiar patterns:

```
var treemap = d3.layout.treemap()
            .size([width, height])
            .padding(3)
            .value(function (d) { return d.count; })
            .sort(d3.ascending);

var nodes = treemap.nodes(tree)
            .filter(function (d) { return d.depth; });
```

We added some padding with `.padding()` to give nodes room to breathe.

Every node will become a group element holding a rectangle. The leaves will also hold a label:

```
var node = svg.selectAll('g')
            .data(nodes)
            .enter()
```

```
            .append('g')
            .classed('node', true)
            .attr('transform', function (d) { return 'translate(
node.a'+d.x+','+d.y+')'; });
```

```
ppend('rect')
        .attr({width: function (d) { return d.dx; },
                height: function (d) { return d.dy; },
                fill: function (d) { return helpers.color(d.nick); }});
```

Now for the first fun bit. Let's fit labels into as many nodes as they can possibly go:

```
var leaves = node.filter(function (d) { return d.depth > 1; });
```

```
    leaves.append('text')
        .text(function (d) { return d.nick; })
        .attr('text-anchor', 'middle')
        .attr('transform', function (d) {
            var box = this.getBBox(),
                transform = 'translate('+(d.dx/2)+','+(d.dy/2+box.
height/2)+')';

            if (d.dx < box.width && d.dx > box.height && d.dy > box.
width) {
                transform += 'rotate(-90)';
            }else if (d.dx < box.width || d.dy < box.height) {
                d3.select(this).remove();
            }

            return transform;
        });
```

Finally! That was some interesting code!

We found all the leaves and started adding text. To fit labels into nodes, we get their size with `this.getBBox()`, then move them to the middle of the node, and check for fit.

If the label is too wide but fits vertically, we rotate it; otherwise, we remove the label after checking again that it doesn't fit. Making sure of the height is important because some nodes are very thin.

We add tooltips with `helpers.tooltip`:

```
        leaves.call(helpers.tooltip
          (function (d) { return d.parent.nick; }));
```

Another fun bit—partially hiding nodes from different parents:

```
leaves.on('mouseover', function (d) {
    var belongs_to = d.parent.nick;

    svg.selectAll('.node')
        .transition()
        .style('opacity', function (d) {
            if (d.depth > 1 && d.parent.nick != belongs_to) {
                return 0.3;
            }
            if (d.depth == 1 && d.nick != belongs_to) {
                return 0.3;
            }
            return 1;
        });
})
    .on('mouseout', function () {
        d3.selectAll('.node')
            .transition()
            .style('opacity', 1);
    });
```

We used two mouse event listeners: one creates the effect, another removes it. The mouseover listener goes through all the nodes and lightens those with a different parent or that aren't the parent (d.parent.nick and d.nick are different). The mouseout listener removes all changes.

After this, add some CSS:

```
<style>
#nicktool {
  font-size: 1.3em;
}

#nicktool rect {
  fill: white;
}

.node text {
  font-size: 0.9em;
}
```

```
.name text {
  font-size: 1.5em;
}

.name rect {
  fill: white;
}
</style>
```

The end result looks like an abstract painting:

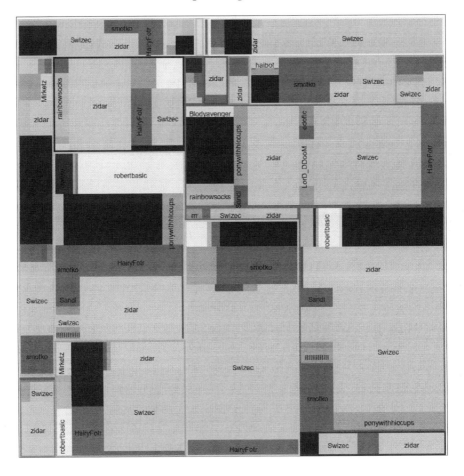

Touching an area with your mouse restores some sanity as shown in the following screenshot:

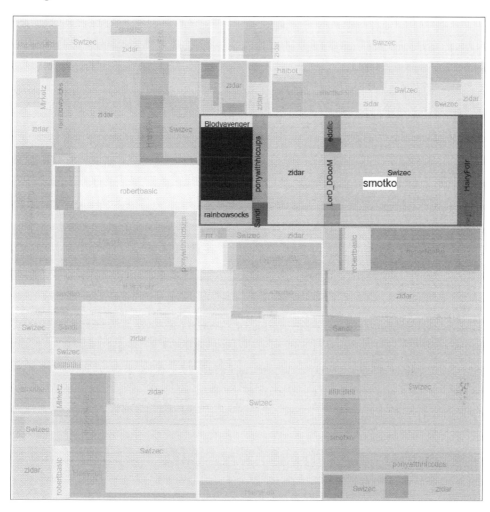

Although, not as much sanity as we hoped.

Summary

Despite the near mythical power of d3 layouts, they turn out to be nothing more than helpers that turn your data into a collection of coordinates.

After going full out with these examples, we used almost every trick we've learned so far. We even wrote so much code that we had to make a separate library! With a bit of generalization, some of those functions could be layouts of their own. There's a whole world of community-developed layouts for various types of charts. The d3-plugins repository on GitHub (`https://github.com/d3/d3-plugins`) is a good way to start exploring.

You now understand what all the default layouts are up to, and I hope you're already thinking about using them for purposes beyond the original developers' wildest dreams.

6
Designing Good Visualizations

A good visualization is not just about having fun with JavaScript. A visualization should tell a story using data and should look good doing it. You want to pull in and intrigue viewers with your aesthetics and expose the world with your story.

To be perfectly honest, this chapter seemed the most difficult one to write. But what sort of book about making beautiful visualizations would this be if we didn't talk about what makes a visualization gorgeous and effective?

I'm a programmer, not a designer, but I've gone through a lot of visualizations, good and bad. Let me show you some I've found amazing.

What is a visualization?

A visualization is just a picture based on data. Any time you take data and turn it into a picture, you've created a visualization.

As *Economic and Industrial Delusions: A Discussion of the Case for Protection, Farquhar, Arthur B* — a classic book from the 19th century — puts it:

> *"The graphical method has considerable superiority for the exposition of statistical facts over the tabular. A heavy bank of figures is grievously wearisome to the eye and the popular mind is as incapable of drawing any useful lessons from it as of extracting sunbeams from cucumbers"*

But there is a world of difference between charts and graphs of old and the visual masterpieces from the examples gallery of d3.js. The new medium lets us do so much more with data that the growth in popularity of visualizations is hardly surprising.

Compared to a good modern visualization, a chart barely goes beyond showing raw data. It doesn't tell you anything, but a visualization does.

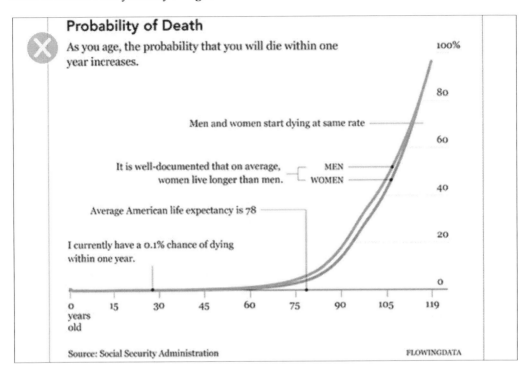

You don't even have to go full out. Sometimes, adding labels is enough to turn a boring graph into an appealing visualization—a trick often used by *The New York Times*.

A simple graph of just two exponentially rising lines: boring. Add some labels and it's a gripping tale. An explanation of what you're seeing placed at the top-left corner of the graph, highlighted story points on the graph, and even the legend comes with an interesting point on the story.

Amanda Cox, a graphics editor for *The New York Times*, calls this the annotation layer. Look her up; she's done some great talks about visualizations.

Contrast this with our visualizations so far. They are interesting and have a good wow effect, but are not very good at conveying a story. They were great as examples and made decent art, but we often just didn't have time to label them properly.

Even better, look at this visualization referenced in d3.js's documentation on stacked layouts.

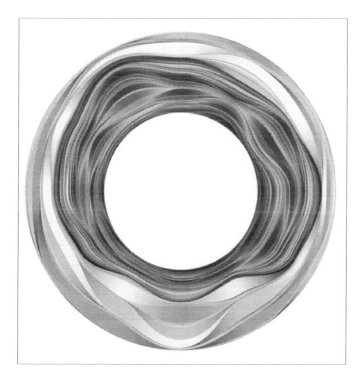

Beautiful! Would you guess that it shows the seasonal ebb and flow of colors in photos from Flickr? Probably not.

With help from a designer, the authors improved this concept for the final print version in *Boston* magazine by labeling the circular time axis and adding typical photos to key points of the image.

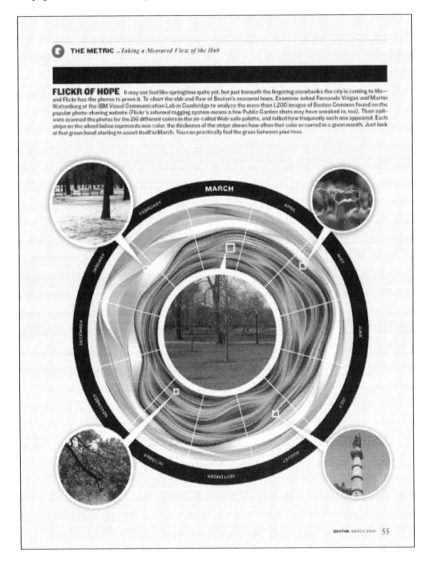

It seems good visualizations find a balance in the happy medium between static charts and data art. A good visualization should be as beautiful as it is informative.

Some great examples

A lot of hard academic research is going into visualization design. Reading some of the material is a great idea when you're looking for something specific—like how best to transition between a scatterplot and a histogram (`http://vis.berkeley.edu/papers/animated_transitions/`)—but coming up to speed on such a vast field takes time.

For an exhaustive look at visualization methods, take a look at the periodic table of visualizations developed by the KPI Library. You can find it at `http://www.visual-literacy.org/periodic_table/periodic_table.html`.

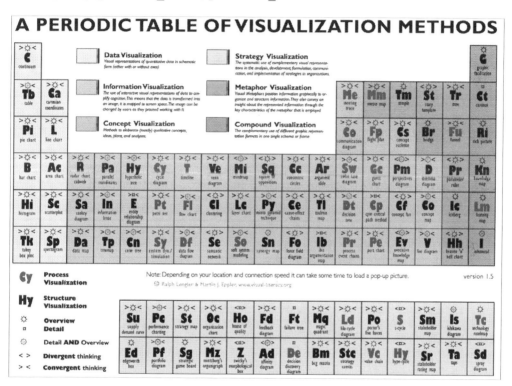

The periodic table uses six categories—**Data**, **Information**, **Concept**, **Strategy**, **Metaphor**, and **Compound** visualization. Hovering over a cell shows an example category.

The table itself is a well-done visualization. It may not be beautiful or artistic, but emulates the common periodic table perfectly. It immediately draws our attention and sticks in our mind because of the familiarity, and presents the data well. On the other hand, there's too much going on and there is no emphasis. Rather than a story, you get a "here's everything; deal with it".

On top of it all, this periodic table is a bitmap image—that's something you should never do on the Web for reasons ranging from search engines to usability.

Riot arrests

How *The Guardian* covered the riot arrests during the 2012 London riots is an example of a simple yet powerful visualization.

Histograms are the obvious choice for comparing category sizes, but you run into the problem of people seeing trends that aren't there. People are also forced to read the labels because all the bars look alike.

Histograms break down further when you want to compare subcategories or they just show the sum of all categories.

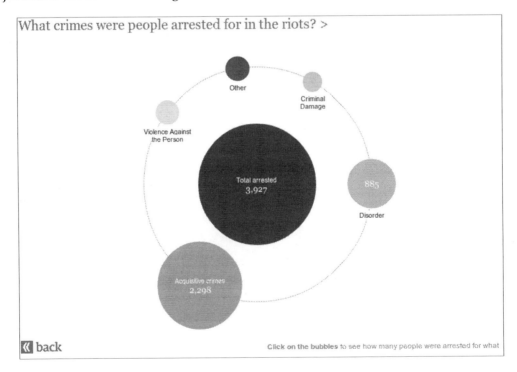

The Guardian used color to differentiate categories and circle area to show the size of these categories. This works because, through years of graphs and charts, everyone's learned that colors are categories. Even before seeing the numbers, readers recognize that a bigger circle is a bigger category. Just be careful to use area to represent values, not diameter—a diameter half as big produces a circle only a quarter as big!

The only information that isn't obvious at a glance is that the smaller circles are subcategories of the central big circle. This question is quickly answered by clicking on any of the smaller circles.

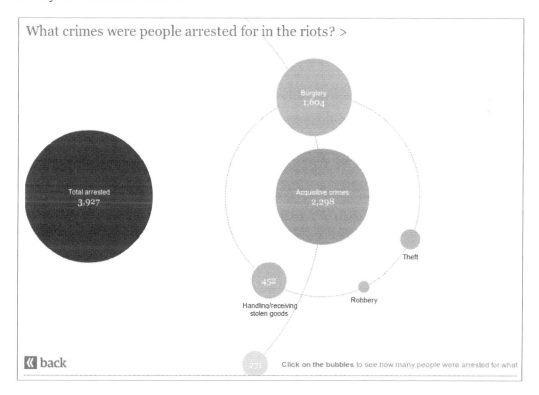

You can find this visualization at http://www.guardian.co.uk/uk/datablog/
interactive/2011/dec/06/england-riots-crimes-arrested.

Les Misérables Co-occurrence

Another great use of color is displaying intensity. This approach is most often used in matrix diagrams where darker means more and lighter means less. It's a very natural effect—empty cells are white, and the more points you put in a cell, the darker it becomes. Try it with a pen.

Mike Bostock used this effect in the Les Misérables diagram that's showing characters appearing in the same chapter.

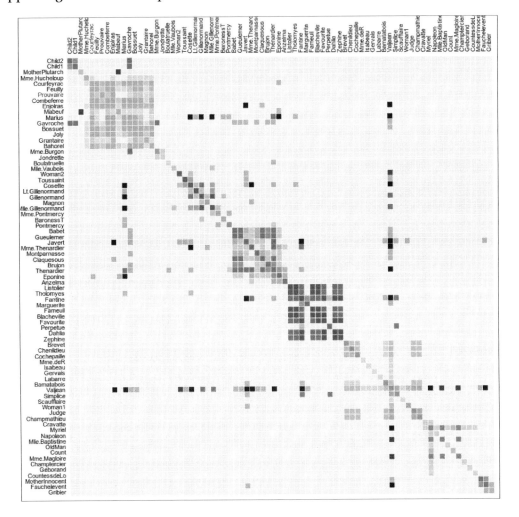

Unlike graphs and trees, matrix diagrams don't become too busy with a lot of connections. Remember our chord diagram, the unreadable jungle of thin connections? That doesn't happen here.

Matrix diagrams are, however, sensitive to edge ordering. When the edges are ordered with a clustering algorithm—community discovery—we get a beautiful picture.

But the matrix looks very different with alphabetical edges.

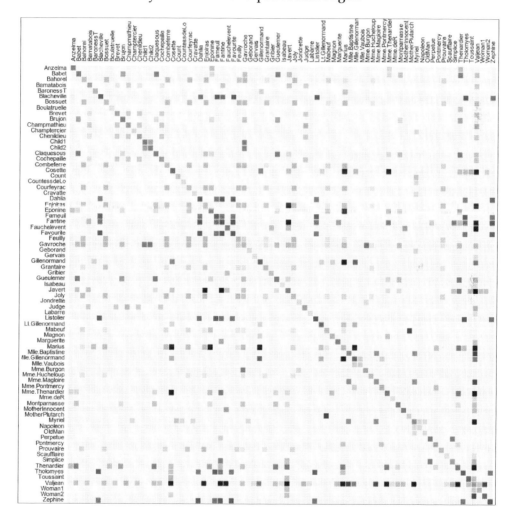

It is a lot messier and paints a worse picture than the clustered version.

Another problem that matrix diagrams suffer from is that following a path between two nodes is almost impossible. Choose your visualization wisely.

You can find the *Les Misérables Co-occurrence* matrix at `http://bost.ocks.org/mike/miserables/`.

The Wealth & Health of Nations

Another interesting problem faced by visualizations is packing too many dimensions into a two-dimensional medium. How would you plot the relationship between per capita income and life expectancy of a nation? A simple line chart, right? But how do you incorporate time, add more nations, population, and... let's add region just to make things interesting. That's five dimensions!

Gapminder's Wealth & Health of Nations is a beautiful example of squeezing five dimensions into two without crowding. Every nation is a bubble on a graph, where the vertical axis shows life expectancy and the horizontal axis is per capita income. Time is shown as time with an animation, regions are colors, and population is circle area.

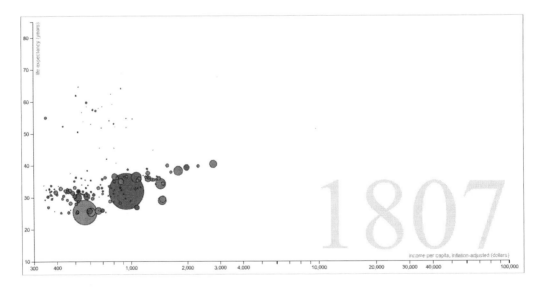

Maybe I get too excited by data, but watching those dots dance around and grow bigger as time goes by is really fun. You can explore histories of whole nations!

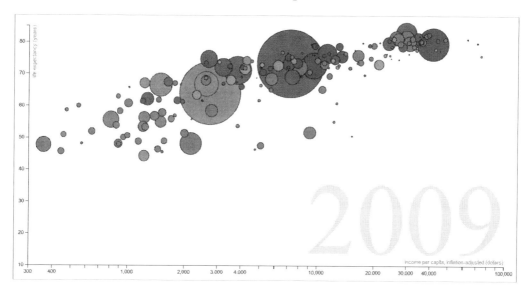

You can see the direct correlation between the wealth of a nation and its life expectancy. Furthermore, everyone's life expectancy goes up and all nations become bigger as time passes.

Another fun game I tried was pinpointing great events in history. Japan, for instance, does a full circle as her wealth and health had plummeted around 1945 but soon recovered.

You can find Mike Bostock's d3.js recreation of the visualization at `http://bost.ocks.org/mike/nations/`.

More great stuff

We could analyze many more examples together, but where's the fun in that? Find your own inspiration on the Internet. The d3.js examples gallery has many gems, such as the airport wind history visualization that uses circular histograms (`http://windhistory.com/map.html#9.00/33.5876/-118.1257`) or drawing of koalas drawn by splitting circles in a fractal pattern: `http://www.koalastothemax.com/`.

The New York Times listing, *2012: The Year in Graphics*, is another great resource. The visualizations about the Olympics are my favorite. They are available at `http://www.nytimes.com/interactive/2012/12/30/multimedia/2012-the-year-in-graphics.html`.

The Guardian publishes a list of their visualizations together with the datasets. You can access it at `http://www.guardian.co.uk/data`.

Summary

We dipped our toes into the design side of things, looked at some great examples, and tried to learn how they work. As a non-designer, that's how I approach any new visualization I want to create—look at a bunch of examples and figure out what works on my dataset.

Then it's experimentation, experimentation, and playing around until I find something that works.

For a deeper look at designing visualizations, I suggest reading books devoted to the subject. *Data Visualization: a successful design process, Andy Kirk* and his blog *Visualizing Data* are a good start. I haven't read the book, but the blog helped me a lot during this chapter.

Another good resource is *Visualize This, Nathan Yau*. The first few chapters are about design; the rest are about using R—a language for statistical analysis. It would also be good to read *Interactive Data Visualization for the Web, Scott Murray*.

Index

Symbols

A

B

C

D

M

map 91
map command 66
M command 43

N

nested transitions 95

O

ordinal scales 76, 78

P

pack layout
  about 158
  using 158
path element
  arc 49, 50
  area 47, 48
  axes 56-58
  chord 52, 53
  diagonal 54, 55
  line 45, 47
  symbol 50, 51
  using 42-44
pie
  partitioning 155, 157
pie chart layout
  using 128-132
play environment
  Chrome Developer Tools, used for tweak-
    ing visualizations 9
  setting up 8
polygons element 30, 37
polylines element 30, 37
punchcard 10
Python 9

Q

quantitative scales
  about 78
  continuous range scales 79, 81
  discrete range scales 81

R

radiate function 106
rectangle element 30, 32, 33
redraw() function 26
reduce function 66
Reingold-Tilford algorithm 151
rotate() transformation 37

S

Scalable Vector Graphics. *See* SVG
scales
  about 74, 75
  ordinal scales 76, 78
  quantitative scales 78
scale() transformation 37
selection
  about 21, 22
  data, joining to 24
  example 22, 23
SimpleHTTPServer module 9
skewX() transformation 37
skewY() transformation 37
spiral function 68, 69
Spirographs 104
stack layout
  about 132
  using 132-139
straight line element 30, 31
streamgraph 133
SVG
  about 19, 29
  drawing with 29
  elements, adding 30
  path element 42, 43, 44
  shapes, adding 30
  transformation 37-42
SVG image 30
symbol 50, 51

T

text element 30
time 83

Thank you for buying
Data Visualization with d3.js

About Packt Publishing

Packt, pronounced 'packed', published its first book "*Mastering phpMyAdmin for Effective MySQL Management*" in April 2004 and subsequently continued to specialize in publishing highly focused books on specific technologies and solutions.

Our books and publications share the experiences of your fellow IT professionals in adapting and customizing today's systems, applications, and frameworks. Our solution based books give you the knowledge and power to customize the software and technologies you're using to get the job done. Packt books are more specific and less general than the IT books you have seen in the past. Our unique business model allows us to bring you more focused information, giving you more of what you need to know, and less of what you don't.

Packt is a modern, yet unique publishing company, which focuses on producing quality, cutting-edge books for communities of developers, administrators, and newbies alike. For more information, please visit our website: www.packtpub.com.

About Packt Open Source

In 2010, Packt launched two new brands, Packt Open Source and Packt Enterprise, in order to continue its focus on specialization. This book is part of the Packt Open Source brand, home to books published on software built around Open Source licences, and offering information to anybody from advanced developers to budding web designers. The Open Source brand also runs Packt's Open Source Royalty Scheme, by which Packt gives a royalty to each Open Source project about whose software a book is sold.

Writing for Packt

We welcome all inquiries from people who are interested in authoring. Book proposals should be sent to author@packtpub.com. If your book idea is still at an early stage and you would like to discuss it first before writing a formal book proposal, contact us; one of our commissioning editors will get in touch with you.

We're not just looking for published authors; if you have strong technical skills but no writing experience, our experienced editors can help you develop a writing career, or simply get some additional reward for your expertise.

Data Visualization: a successful design process

ISBN: 978-1-849693-46-2   Paperback: 206 pages

A structured design approach to equip you with the knowledge of how to successfully accomplish any data visualization challenge efficiently and effectively

1. A portable, versatile and flexible data visualization design approach that will help you navigate the complex path towards success

2. Explains the many different reasons for creating visualizations and identifies the key parameters which lead to very different design options

3. Thorough explanation of the many visual variables and visualization taxonomy to provide you with a menu of creative options

MATLAB Graphics and Data Visualization Cookbook

ISBN: 978-1-849693-16-5   Paperback: 284 pages

Tell data stories with compelling graphics using this collection of data visualization recipes

1. Collection of data visualization recipes with functionalized versions of common tasks for easy integration into your data analysis workflow

2. Recipes cross-referenced with MATLAB product pages and MATLAB Central File Exchange resources for improved coverage

3. Includes hand created indices to find exactly what you need; such as application driven, or functionality driven solutions

Please check **www.PacktPub.com** for information on our titles

Instant Heat Maps in R How-to

ISBN: 978-1-782165-64-4   Paperback: 72 pages

Learn how to design heat maps in R to enhance your data analysis

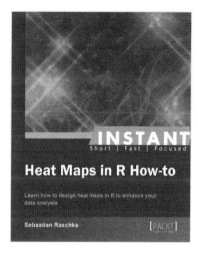

1. Learn something new in an Instant!
    A short, fast, focused guide delivering immediate results

2. Create heat maps in R using different file formats

3. Learn how to make choropleth maps and contour plots

4. Generate your own customized heat maps and add interactivity for displaying on the web

Google Visualization API Essentials

ISBN: 978-1-849694-36-0   Paperback: 252 pages

Make sense of your data: make it visual with the Google Visualization API

1. Wrangle all sorts of data into a visual format, without being an expert programmer

2. Visualize new or existing spreadsheet data through charts, graphs, and maps

3. Full of diagrams, core concept explanations, best practice tips, and links to working book examples

Please check **www.PacktPub.com** for information on our titles

27633845R00105

Made in the USA
Lexington, KY
17 November 2013

Data Visualization with d3.js

d3.js provides a platform that helps you create beautiful visualization and brings data to life using HTML, SVG, and CSS. It emphasizes on web standards that will fully utilize the capabilities of your web browser.

The book begins with the basics of putting lines on the screen, and builds on this foundation all the way to creating interactive animated visualizations using d3.js layouts.

You will learn how to use d3.js to manipulate vector graphics with SVG, layout with HTML, and styling with CSS. You'll take a look at the basics of functional programming and using data structures effectively – everything from handling time to doing geographic projections. The book will alsohelp make your visualizations interactive and teach you how automated layouts really work.

Data Visualization with d3.js will unveil the mystery behind all those beautiful examples you've been admiring.

Who this book is written for

This book is ideal for anyone interested in data visualization. Some rudimentary knowledge of JavaScript is required.

What you will learn from this book

- Draw with SVG shapes and path generators

- Add styles with HTML and CSS

- Use data structures effectively

- Dynamically update visualizations as data changes

- Animate visualizations

- Let the user explore your data

- Use layouts to create complex drawings

- Learn to identify what makes a good visualization better

$ 29.99 US
£ 18.99 UK

Prices do not include
local sales tax or VAT
where applicable

ISBN 978-1-78216-000-7

52999

9 781782 160007

PUBLISHING

open source*
community experience distilled

Visit **www.PacktPub.com** for books, eBooks,
code, downloads, and PacktLib.